Information Technology for the Small Business

How to make IT work for your company

T.J. Benoit

Library of Congress Cataloging-in-Publication Data

Benoit, Thomas A. Jr. (TJ) 1960-

Information Technology for the Small Business / TJ Benoit
Includes Index
ISBN 0-9785672-0-X

Cover Design: Joshua Drumm
Editors: Holly Boutwell, Michael Gubetta, Marcia Harriman
Graphics: T.J. Benoit, Joshua Drumm
Photography: Carmine Filloramo, TAB® file photos

E-mail: tj@tabinc.com

All trademarks contained in this publication are the property of their respective companies. If any items appear to be a trademarked name, please research to determine the proper trademark owner.

TAB® and PatrolDog® are licensed trademarks of TAB® Computer Systems, Inc.

No portion of this publication may be reproduced or transmitted in any form or by any means, graphic, electronic, or mechanical, including photocopying, recording, taping, or by any information storage retrieval system, without the prior written permission of TAB Computer Systems, Inc. 29-31 Bissell St., East Hartford, CT 06108

Printed in the United States of America

This publication is sold with the understanding that the publisher is not engaged in rendering legal or accounting professional services. If legal advice or other expert assistance is required, the services of a competent professional person should be sought.

**Copyright © 2006 TAB Computer Systems, Inc.
All rights reserved.**

TABLE OF CONTENTS

ABOUT THE AUTHOR V

PREFACE VII

WHAT IS INFORMATION TECHNOLOGY? 1

THE BASICS 2
   PC/Workstation 2
   Software 6
   Network Environment 8
      Internet Protocol (IP) 11

THE SMALL BUSINESS 12
   The Small Business Owner 12
   How Big Are You? 15
   How Dependent Are You? 16

WHO'S ON MY TEAM? 19
   Outside Helpers and Contributors 20
   Outside Vendors 23
   What to Look for in Local IT Services 26
      Common Technician Certifications 28
   Who Else is on My Team? 29
      Employees 29
      Owner 30

WHAT DOES IT COST? 31
   Annual Cost Calculations 32
   Total Cost of Ownership 34
   Return on Investment 35

i

THE 10 MOST CRITICAL IT PITFALLS **36**

PROTECT YOUR BUSINESS **39**
   Keep Up with Current Technology - Carefully 39
   Implement Application Software Upgrades with Care 40

Educate Your Employees About Your IT Policy **42**

Employee Training **44**
   Local IT Training Venues 45
   Skill Set Profile 46

Application Software **48**

YOUR IT TEAM **53**

GET IT ORGANIZED!! **54**
   Administrator's Handbook 54
   Emergency Contact List 55
   User Profile Sheet 56
   ROUTER/Gateway/ISP Information Sheet 59

File Server Folder Structure **61**

File Naming Conventions **63**
   Changing File Associations 66

Asset Listing/Photos **67**

Digital Cameras **68**

Software Organization and Storage **69**

PUTTING IT TOGETHER **72**

YOUR NETWORK **73**

Critical Equipment Location/Placement **75**
   Optimal Scenario 76
   Acceptable/Minimum Scenario 77
   Unacceptable/Potentially Dangerous Scenario 78

THE INTERNET - YOUR BUSINESS ONLINE **80**
   Domain Names 80

Your Company Web Site 81
Web Site "Uptime" 82
What to Look for in a Web Designer 83

E-mail in Your Business 85
How E-mail Works 86
E-mail Names 86
E-mail Subject 87
E-mail Etiquette 87
E-mail Protection/Backup 88
E-mail Organization 89
SPAM Filtering 92

Web Browsers 93

Internet User Names and Passwords 97
Shared Passwords – Not Secured 99
Password Changes 99

BACKUP YOUR DATA 100
Continuous Data Protection Servers (CDP) 104
Workstation Imaging 105
Disaster Recovery Planning 108

DISASTER PREVENTION PLANNING 110
Terminated Employees 111
Disposal of Data 112
Charitable Donations/Computer Recycling 114

FILE SERVER – WHY DO I NEED ONE? 115
File Server Software 117
Remote Server Monitoring 118

POWER – HOW IMPORTANT IS IT? 120

WORKSTATION SPECIFICATIONS 123

THE WRAP UP 126

QUICK REFERENCE 128

iii

Basic Installation Considerations **129**
Quick PC Troubleshooting Guide **131**
In-Depth PC Troubleshooting Guide **133**
Internet Troubleshooting Guide **136**
Browser Troubleshooting Guide **138**
Troubleshooting Tips for Other Scenarios **139**
   Multiple office computers that cannot receive or send e-mail...................... 139
   Multiple office computers and only one cannot send and/or receive e-mail. 139
   Local Printer Won't Print 140
Installing a Windows Printer Driver **141**
   USB Printers (Windows 98 and newer) 141
   Parallel Port Printers (Windows XP) 142
Making a Backup Copy of Your E-mail Data **143**
   Backing Up Microsoft Outlook Express Data.. 143
   Backing Up Microsoft Outlook Data (without Exchange)............................ 143
   Backing Up Additional Outlook Information 144

GLOSSARY **145**

BIBLIOGRAPHY **151**

INDEX **154**

iv

About the Author

T.J. Benoit has been integrating small business owners with information technology since 1983 when he designed his first order entry PC program for a costume manufacturer. His knowledge of computers extends from mainframe programming (Travelers Insurance Company) in the late 1970's, to System 36/38 and AS/400 platforms, as well as Novell, Microsoft and Apple software. He has developed hundreds of applications specifically used in business environments, ranging from Accounting to Medical and Collections systems. His "NetClean+" software application won "Shareware Pick of the Year" in 1994, and was featured in "Computer Shopper." His "PatrolDog" server monitor software was included in November 2005 *Microsoft TechNet* article on emerging software.

TAB Computer Systems, Inc. (TAB) was started in his basement in 1983. TAB now has more than 1,500 small business clients in the New England area. T.J. continues to be active in all facets of TAB's daily operations. He was selected as a "Forty Under 40" designee in 1999 in recognition for the growth of his small business, and was twice nominated for "Small IT Business of the Year" by the Hartford Area Chamber of Commerce.

He has served on the advisory board for curriculum at Goodwin College in East Hartford, CT. He lectures and speaks on current IT topics for computer user groups, and at local colleges. He is an active Rotarian, and a Paul Harris Fellow, recognized by Rotary International for his dedication to public service. He has served as a Rotarian officer in every capacity, including President.

He has written weekly columns for the *New Britain Herald Press* and contributes to various sites about information technology and specific development platforms. His articles on the "Communications Decency Act" have been published by the American Library Association and quoted in other publications.

Since 1995, he has been the co-host of "Computer Talk with TAB," a weekly talk radio show heard on WTIC-AM 1080. He fields thousands of technology and business questions during the course of a year. He is also frequently called upon as an industry expert for IT issues and their business impact for other talk radio shows and television.

T.J. is married with three children and resides in the Hartford, CT area.

Courtesy: Carmine Filloramo Photography

PREFACE

I've been building a small business since 1983. I started out on my own, in my basement, programming for a single client and continued that way for about six years, adding clients along the way. I hired my first employee in 1989 and was, then, truly a "small business." Like most cautious entrepreneurs, I've grown my business very slowly, and made many "corrections" and path changes along the way.

One area, however, in which I've always invested appropriate planning and resources, is Information Technology (IT). As I was assisting other businesses, I was also learning what **not** to do in the IT area. This strategy has been invaluable to me, and my clients, over the years, and has provided many of the tips and strategies detailed in this book.

Coming from a corporate background, I realized from the start, that while "Corporate America" is fraught with elaborate and expensive techniques, they also have all the IT basics completely defined and implemented. These fundamentals should (and must) be carried into the small business arena because they simply make sense when dealing with IT processes. This is the area that is most often overlooked – the "basics" of Information Technology. It is my sincere hope that this book will be a valuable tool and resource for all small business owners, equipping them with knowledge and benefits from my experience. You need to cover the basics – exactly what this book will address.

When I originally embarked on this writing project, I intended to write a series of "Self-Help" or "How-To" booklets that would assist TAB clients in understanding IT-related tasks such as the importance of daily backups, server maintenance, etc. As I cataloged and developed the list of topics, I realized that for every short article I wrote, I needed to reference related areas in more detail in order to help the reader visualize and comprehend the total picture and "make sense of it all." That's when I realized that I needed to, in fact, write a book.

By the way, I'm still building that business 23 years later - where each day is a constant challenge and every night is still a worry! Welcome to small business ownership. I'm hoping that I can ease the burden and offer some guidance in the IT arena.

If you are a small business owner who uses IT and PC's to perform daily tasks in your business, **this book is for you**.

If you don't really know that much about computers and technology, but you supervise and coordinate people who use them daily, **this book is for you**.

If you are in charge of purchasing IT equipment, even occasionally, and need assistance with purchasing specifications and guidance, **this book is for you.**

Most of all......

If you are trying to earn a living in business and are confused by all this "computer stuff," **this book is for you.**

I'll do my best to help you understand the right questions to ask and, perhaps just as importantly, the right answers to expect. I'll provide the guidance and confidence you'll need to make IT work for your small business.

Acknowledgements

I'd like to thank the people who gave me input during the editing of this book: Holly Boutwell, Rich Carlson, Michael Gubetta, Marcia Harriman, John Moran, Tony Velez, Josh Drumm and Carmine Filloramo. It was their valuable input that made this a better book. This book is dedicated to my wife Maryanne, who supports me and every one of my endeavors, all the time.

T.J.
June 2006

What is Information Technology?

The American Heritage Dictionary defines Information Technology (IT) as *"the development, installation, and implementation of computer systems and applications."* While this is technically accurate, IT has grown in scope to have increasingly broad-reaching effect on both business and everyday personal life.

A successful small business utilizes IT on a daily basis. This book will focus on the most critical IT aspects for the efficient and growth-oriented small business owner. As we navigate through the IT process, certain aspects will be analyzed in a detailed and comprehensive manner, while others will be presented in a more general overview.

> *Information Technology: "...a term that encompasses all forms of technology used to create, store, exchange, and use information in its various forms...."*

Because the IT scope is so comprehensive and far-reaching, this book will focus on core areas that have direct impact on your business:

- The "Basics" of Information Technology
- Operating Systems
- Backups/Data Protection/Security
- Application Software
- E-mail
- The Internet and the World Wide Web
- Computer Hardware
- Troubleshooting Common Problems

The Basics

In order to establish a usable foundation of just what is involved in IT, let's begin by looking at the various IT components. At a basic level, IT is comprised of hardware (what's left when there is no electricity), software (which runs on the hardware and performs tasks for you), and networks (a combination of both hardware and software that interconnects with other hardware and software).

Your business is undoubtedly already using all three IT components to various degrees and, perhaps, to different degrees of efficiency. One of the primary goals of this book is to assist you in determining where your business is in terms of IT configuration. We will not be delving into great detail on these concepts, however. Our focus will be more of a "view from 10,000 feet" to get you, as the small business owner, comfortable with the "lingo" without getting bogged down in the details.

PC/Workstation

Today's personal computer (PC or workstation) is a highly sophisticated piece of equipment. The computing power in the average PC today is roughly equivalent to a multi-million dollar supercomputer of just a decade ago. Most PC users don't really know what's inside their PC; they simply use it to do their job. This section is for those curious about just what is inside the average PC. Here's a component list:

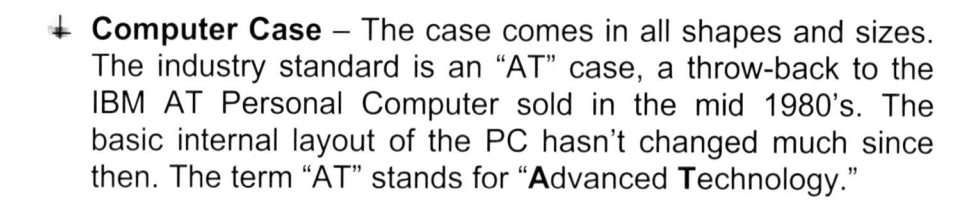

- **Computer Case** – The case comes in all shapes and sizes. The industry standard is an "AT" case, a throw-back to the IBM AT Personal Computer sold in the mid 1980's. The basic internal layout of the PC hasn't changed much since then. The term "AT" stands for "**A**dvanced **T**echnology."

- **Power Supply** – The power supply provides power to all internal components. The average power supply in today's PC is approximately 300-400 watts of output. The power supply is called a "DC supply" because it converts AC (**A**lternating **C**urrent from your wall outlet) at 120 volts into DC (**D**irect **C**urrent) at around 12 volts. This power is then fed to the rest of the machine.

- **Motherboard** – The motherboard is the "heart" of the PC. All PC components interact in some way with the motherboard. The main components that reside on or in the motherboard are:

    - **Processor** – The processor is the "brains" of the PC. Frequently, the processor is referred to as Intel Pentium III, Intel Pentium IV, AMD Athlon, etc. These are all processor brand names, also known as CPU or **C**entral **P**rocessing **U**nit. The faster the processor measured in Gigahertz, generally the better the performance. The higher the Gigahertz number, the faster the processor.

    - **Memory** – Memory is where the processor stores data while performing operations. For instance, if you are composing a letter in Microsoft Word™, the data appearing on the screen is being temporarily held in Memory (aka RAM – **R**andom **A**ccess **M**emory). If power is lost, or the PC freezes, this data is generally lost. Data is generally not written back out of this area until you "save" it.

        Memory is also where the nucleus, or kernel, of the operating system (OS) is stored. The PC would not operate without this basic frame. When a PC is booted, parts of the operating system load into RAM, where they remain until the PC is powered down.

        More memory is generally better. A workstation running Windows XP™ should have a minimum of 512 megabytes. A file server should have no less than one gigabyte of memory.

- **Additional Interfaces** – Almost all motherboards currently contain additional components integrated directly onto them. Industry refers to them as "on board interfaces" or "on board controllers."

    o **Network Interface** – The network interface is how the computer communicates with an outside network, such as the Internet. The connection looks like an oversized phone jack, actually called an RJ-45 connector.

    o **USB Interface** – The **U**niversal **S**erial **B**us interface is quickly becoming the standard for all peripheral devices such as printers, scanners, PDA's (Personal Digital Assistants), etc. The connector is rectangular. There are normally at least two USB connectors in a computer.

    o **Parallel Interface** – This 36-pin connection is used to communicate with printers. It has not been widely used since the introduction of USB-based printers.

    o **Serial Interface** – This 9-pin connection is rarely used in present computer configurations. As with the parallel interface, it has been largely replaced by USB.

    o **Video Display Interface** – This interface is used to supply the video output from a computer. Many high-end computers will add internal additional cards to replace this interface in order to get better performance and better graphics.

- **Hard Drive** – This device stores data on a more permanent basis. When data is saved, it is generally written to a PC hard drive. Today's hard drives are measured in gigabytes, or Gigs, looking like this: 1,000,000,000 bytes (a byte is 1 character of information). The average hard drive today is, at minimum, 80 gigabytes in size. This is a tremendous amount of storage capacity and will only increase going forward. For reference, 80 Gigs will hold 27,000 MP3 audio songs or approximately 80,000 digital photographs. It's a tremendous amount of storage space!

- **CD-ROM** – CD-ROM (**C**ompact **D**isk **R**ead **O**nly **M**emory) drives may contain up to 650 megabytes of data and/or music. That's approximately two-thirds of a gigabyte. Common uses for CD's include installing software or copying data and music.

- **DVD-ROM** – DVD-ROM (**D**igital **V**ideo **D**isc **R**ead **O**nly **M**emory) is a newer format that may contain up to 4.3 Gigabytes of data ("dual layer" DVD can hold twice that amount). This is also a very popular movie format as well. Most movies available for rent at Blockbuster or Netflix are in a DVD format. As technology improves, this format will hold increasingly more data. As with CD-ROM, the advantage for using this media for storage is its archival factor. Because the data is stored on a piece of plastic, it has a shelf life of more than 50 years, making it ideal for long-term backups.

> **TIP** *If you own only one PC, consider DVD as a backup media choice.*

- **Monitor** – The output screening device that allows the user to see what the computer is doing. There are many types of monitors, available at different price levels.

- **Keyboard** – The primary way to communicate with the computer.

- **Mouse** – The pointing device to identify and select items on the screen.

Software

Computer software comes in many forms. Software can, for instance, be used as an operating system, forming the stepping stone for all other software to operate. It may also be used as an "Application" to perform various computer tasks. Software may even be used for games and just for having computer fun.

Over the past 20 years, no other company has dominated the software market more than Microsoft. They provide the operating systems such as Windows 2000 and Windows XP for more than 93% of PCs worldwide, and provide 55% of the network operating system software as well. Their "Office" application suite and its components such as Microsoft Word, Excel, PowerPoint and Access are used by more than 90% of all businesses in the world using this type of software. Their "Internet Explorer" browser enjoys a 90%+ market share as well. In short, Microsoft has the market covered.

When software is originally purchased, it generally comes in CD form along with a license of some sort. As will be detailed in subsequent chapters, it's critical to store the software and licensing information safely. Software, especially for an operating system, often requires "patches" and "hot fixes" to be installed to remedy various issues discovered after the software originally shipped. For instance, if your operating system continually freezes when attempting to print, it could indicate a possible software issue. If enough users experience this same problem, software companies may issue corrected software. There's no need to release every part of the program, rather, just some pieces.

In the Microsoft world, minimal fixes are called "hot fixes" or "patches." Major groups of fixes are called "Service Packs." A Service Pack is generally cumulative – that is, all new versions of software are contained in every service pack. To Microsoft, this differs from "Service Releases" which are not cumulative, but rather need to be installed in the order they were released. Some application software companies also use the term "PTF" (**P**rogram

Temporary Fix) or simply "System Updates." In instances when the entire program is replaced, it's usually called a "new release."

The other types of software that can cause confusion among computer users are "drivers." Drivers are special programs that provide a common interface between a piece of hardware and the operating system. Think of them as an "interpreter" that translates communication into a common language. For instance, a printer driver is supplied with a printer, usually on CD. This driver tells the operating system how to make it work, what it looks like, whether it is color capable, etc. It also allows the user to see what is going on with the printer on the computer screen and to interact with the device.

> **QUOTE** *Who cares how it works, just as long as it gives the right answer! - Jeff Scholnik*

Network Environment

It is possible to utilize network infrastructures using the Internet with only one PC. Basically, only a limited knowledge of networks is necessary for a user to be able to access the Internet. The environment with more than one PC is only slightly more complicated.

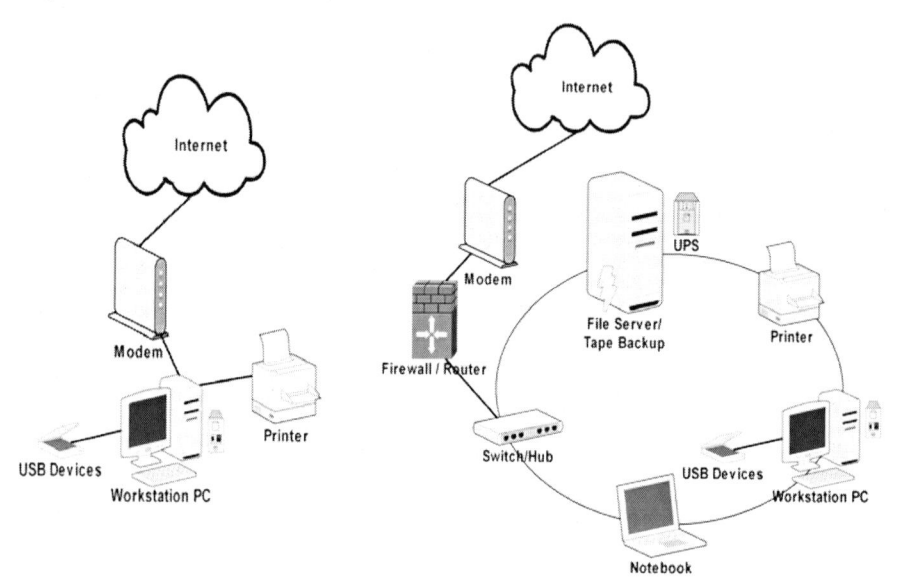

In a typical small office environment, there are essentially 9 major network components. There may be many devices, but they fall into the following component categories:

Component	Description	Average
File Server w/Tape Backup	This computer is responsible for the central storage of company data. It allows users to share data across a network without the need to copy them, e-mail, etc. As the caretaker of critical company data, it also contains a tape backup unit for data archiving.	1

Component	Description	Average
Modem	The modem can be dial up, DSL or Cable flavored. The modem speaks directly to the ISP (Internet Service Provider) and maintains contact with them.	1
Firewall/Router	This device communicates with the modem and acts as a funnel to move data from/to the outside world. It also can act as a wall between the file server and the outside world, keeping unwanted visitors out of the network. It may also contain inside configuration information that makes the device work properly. The device is often referred to as the "gateway" out of the network. An IT professional can access this valuable information when necessary.	1
Cables	These act as "pipes" to allow the flow of data from computer to computer. Cables come in many flavors, including RJ-45 Ethernet, USB, Parallel, Serial, VGA (Video), FireWire, etc.	Many
Switches or Hubs	These devices control the flow of data on the network, getting it from point A to point B, and then safely back again. Some are referred to as "smart" or "managed" because they will "learn" to move data in the most efficient manner possible.	1
Personal Computers (PCs)	These are the network workhorses used to do company work. PC internals were profiled earlier.	2-50

Component	Description	Average
Printers	These come in many shapes, sizes and flavors, but all of them essentially print on a blank piece of paper.	1-3
UPS Devices	**U**ninterruptible **P**ower **S**upplies should always be used between each PC and the wall power source to protect against the possibility that a power outage could damage or shut down your network.	1 per PC and Server
USB Devices, i.e., Palm Pilots, iPods, etc.	These devices, known as "peripherals," are add-ons to the basic computer system.	

> **QUOTE** *"I have always wished that my computer would be as easy to use as my telephone. My wish has come true. I no longer know how to use my telephone." -- Bjarne Stroustrup, inventor of the C++ language.*

There will be discussions and references to these network components throughout the book. Although this sample is a microcosm of a network, it accurately represents a network with two users as much as it does a network with 20,000 users. The only variable is the number of devices involved.

Internet Protocol (IP)

All network computers that wish to "talk" with one another must speak the same language. The accepted language in use today is "TCP/IP" (**T**ransmission **C**ontrol **P**rotocol / **I**nternet **P**rotocol). All computers accessing the Internet, and each other, use a unique number or IP address that gives every device a unique identity. The protocol flexibility is a major factor in the Internet's expansion.

In order to communicate with each other, computers exchange packets of information. There are checks and balances within the communication to verify that everything arrived properly and in the correct order. The network is also fairly smart, in that it learns who is on its local network, i.e., the office computers, and who is not. If computer "A" gets a request from computer "B," and it knows that computer "B" is not local, it attempts to contact computer "B" via a gateway, usually a router or firewall, to the outside world.

When a computer is added to a network, this type of information generally needs to be defined. Most of this can automatically be done using "DHCP" (**D**ynamic **H**ost **C**onfiguration **P**rotocol). In fact, most Internet Providers use DHCP exclusively to assign these values to computers being attached to a network.

The "Internet" chapter will delve in more detail how names are resolved on the Internet, what domains are, and other interesting aspects of Internet operation.

The Small Business

A small business, by definition, generally produces up to $2 million dollars in annual sales. The Small Business Administration further breaks down small businesses, using SIC codes so, while your precise business classification may vary a bit, let's assume, for discussion purposes, that your business produces approximately $2 million or less in annual sales.

Since this figure represents almost 90% of American businesses, it seems a very viable and important group to discuss. Within each small business, there is a need to look at the single person who has initiated the business. He or she is the "small business owner," the one who has stepped up to the plate. They are willing to accept financial and legal responsibility and are the ones who ultimately win or lose based on what happens in their business.

The Small Business Owner

You, the small business owner, are an entrepreneur and risk taker. You'll work 70-hour weeks and 16-hour days when necessary. You spend so much time and energy working at building your business; you barely have time to keep up with daily events, much less the world of IT. However, as with everything in your business, you try your best to stay current with what's necessary.

> **QUOTE** *"Information technology and business are becoming inextricably interwoven. I don't think anybody can talk meaningfully about one without the talking about the other." – Bill Gates*

If you are like most people in the small business world, you have slowly replaced older methods of information business activities with new, more technologically advanced methods. While the more advanced methods may have initially seemed foreign and awkward when first implemented, they became routine and second nature as time passed. This has both benefits and drawbacks. The benefit is that your company has moved into new IT for daily business use. However, IT that is improperly planned and implemented can ultimately damage your business and, at the very least, cause inefficiency and insecure data. In more severe instances, businesses can experience employee attrition, loss of customers and revenue, legal issues, and can even go out of business if IT is not properly implemented and communicated.

Here is a simple example using a word processing program on a PC that illustrates the point. Before IT, a typewriter would have been used to prepare an Accounts Payable Summary for distribution to staff. The Summary was copied, distributed to appropriate staff, and the original was placed in a file folder for later reference. If retrieval was necessary, the Summary was simply pulled out of the folder from a secure file drawer. Simple enough, right? Now, introduce IT. The Summary is typed into a word processor and necessary copies are printed for distribution, or even e-mailed. The document is saved by clicking that little "disk" icon and the PC stores it.... somewhere.

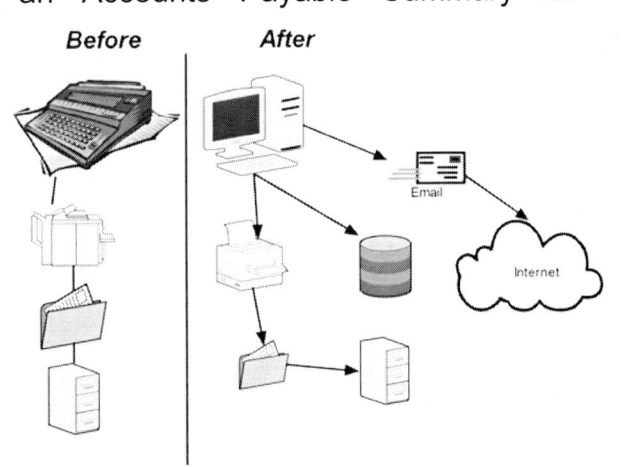

If a deliberate and well-thought-out plan for data storage and retrieval hasn't been developed and communicated within your business, the Summary will almost surely be lost in the abyss of documents. Perhaps, more importantly, the Summary, with sensitive and confidential information, may be in jeopardy of being copied and read by anyone smart enough to access your network.

This includes access from anywhere on earth through a simple Internet connection, as well as direct access from within your own company. In addition, without proper backup in the event of a disk failure, the Summary may be lost forever.

This simple scenario is only one example of the underlying and systematic problems that plague many business owners and employees as they adopt and implement new IT. Why? As with any capital investment, you need to properly plan for its use, and then use it the way it was intended to be used.

Imagine coming to work one morning and **every** PC in your office wouldn't boot up. What would your staff do? Would they be able to perform their job functions? Let's assume that this PC problem was unsolvable for an entire week. How much would this cost your company, both in terms of dollars and customer satisfaction? Would orders be shipped? Would customer correspondence be handled? What about payroll? How about Accounts Payable and Accounts Receivable? Without proper planning, this could be a very bleak picture, with potentially catastrophic consequences—all avoidable. Later, a dependence analysis chart will be introduced as a tool to accurately assess your exposure.

You will read examples throughout this book of real-life scenarios where improper planning and execution caused businesses to lose astounding amounts of dollars and customer credibility. The total impact of poor or non-existent IT planning, just like the need for life insurance, only becomes real for some when disaster strikes!

> QUOTE "You can't buy life insurance once you die." - Anonymous

In many instances, small business owners tend to view IT as a necessary evil and/or an unnecessary expense. Owners may not really embrace IT simply because they don't understand it. As an avoidance technique, they frequently delegate the entire IT planning and direction to an office manager or bookkeeper, who may already be too busy and perhaps not qualified to assume this critical task.

In other instances, the business owner will hire a consultant to assist with the various and complex IT issues, or may even resort to involving friends and family members who are in the IT field to lend a hand. This book addresses all these scenarios in order to help lay an IT framework for your small business.

In the following chapters, we'll begin to build and carefully define your company profile. We'll identify your exposure and, most of all, recommend ways to protect your business from potential and avoidable issues.

How Big Are You?

In the IT world, we define a small business as any business with 50 or fewer PCs and no in-house IT staff on the company payroll. We then categorize each business into one of four classifications, based on average size. Remember, the labels below "Single," "Small," "Medium," and "Large" are relative to the small-business arena only. You'll hear the term "Enterprise" used when discussing larger networks of hundreds or thousands of computers.

Interestingly, we have found that **what** the computers are used for within the network almost always correspond to the number of computers on the network, excluding data acquisition units and retail registers. Simply, the more computers in use, the more the business tends to use them for daily operations.

Single Computer – Used for accounting and some light word processing with e-mail/Internet.

Small Network – Two to five computers, used for a specific application package, accounting, word processing and e-mail/Internet. A file server may be present.

Medium Network – Consists of six to twenty-five computers, used for a combination of tasks, including application software, accounting, office suite software and Internet/e-mail and possibly remote access. A file server is always present.

Large Network – Twenty-six to fifty computers, used for many tasks, including application software, office suite software, Internet/e-mail, large amounts of printing, and remote access. Usually, multiple file servers are in use.

For planning purposes, decide which category best describes your business. We'll refer to this again later.

How Dependent Are You?

In order to determine your business dependence on IT, take a moment to consider the questions below. Rate the following on a scale of 1 to 5, with 1 being "not a problem" and 5 being "critical." Then, identify the number of employees affected if each service were not available for them to do their job for an **entire day**. Total the Rating Column and enter it in the "Daily Total" box.

Dependency Test

Service Area	Rating	Employees
Customer Correspondence – E-mail		
Customer Correspondence – Print Documents		
Accounting (Payables/Receivables)		
Applications (shop floor software, etc.)		
Vendor Access via Internet Web Site		
Internal Correspondence – E-mail		
Shipping Department		
Receiving Department		
Internet Access – General		
Sales/Marketing – Quoting & Contacts		
Daily Total:		

1=No Problem   **2**=Slight Problem   **3**=Moderate Problem   **4**=Serious Problem   **5**=Critical Problem

What if each service below was unavailable for an **entire week?** Total the Rating Column and place it in the "Weekly Total" box.

Service Area	Rating	Employees
Customer Correspondence – E-mail		
Customer Correspondence – Print Documents		
Accounting (Payables/Receivables)		
Applications (shop floor software, etc.)		
Vendor Access via Internet Web Site		
Internal Correspondence – E-mail		
Shipping Department		
Receiving Department		
Internet Access – General		
Sales/Marketing – Quoting & Contacts		
Weekly Total:		

1=No Problem 2=Slight Problem 3=Moderate Problem 4=Serious Problem 5=Critical Problem

Using the "Weekly Total", refer to the Dependence Analysis Chart below.

Total	Weekly Dependence Factor
35 – 50	High Dependence – business continuity in jeopardy
26 – 34	Medium Dependence – could "limp along"
15 – 25	Low Dependence – business would continue to run
< 15	No Dependence

Simply, the higher the score, the more closely IT functions should be managed in your business. In fact, a score of 35 or higher, combined with an IT failure, could indicate a business possibly in jeopardy due to lost production, customers, etc.

If your company placed in the High or Medium dependence range, compare your Daily Factor to the Weekly Factor. You'll probably notice that there is not five times the dependence when comparing the Daily factor to an entire week. More likely, it's about two times greater[+]. This would indicate that even on a daily basis, you are more dependent than you realize.

Using the "Employees" column, total the number of employees affected by the lack of availability and multiply by 40. That is the total loss in production work hours that will need to be made up when the systems are available. Of course, the outages described could affect the same employee multiple times, so the total number may be inflated. However, it should be a large enough number to get you to think about the "what if" part of this example!

Down Time Calculator:
Application Failure: Lost Hours * Overhead Cost per Employee * # of Users
Example: (8 hours * $25.00) * 10 = **$2,000 daily lost production**

[+] based on a random sample of Dependency tests

Who's On My Team?

You are a small business owner and not, by anyone's standards, an "IT guy." You utilize the technology found in computing, but you don't really understand it. You'd like to better understand how it all works, but don't have much time or energy to devote to learning. Your office has become increasingly dependent on IT tools and you're feeling as though you've lost control because you don't know enough.

If this sounds familiar, this book will answer many of your questions and put you on the path to a clearer understanding of the IT world and how it can benefit your small business. Remember, computers and information technologies are just "tools of the trade." Just as

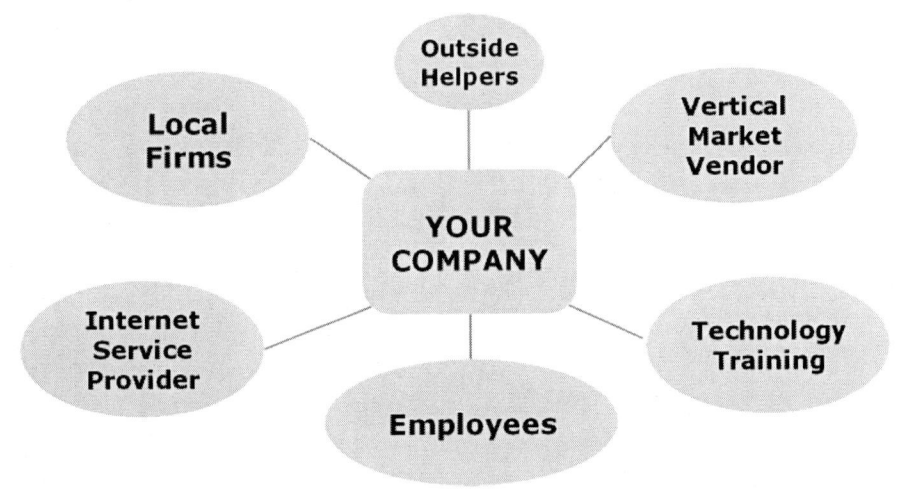

```
              Outside
              Helpers
    Local                     Vertical
    Firms                     Market
                              Vendor
              YOUR
              COMPANY
    Internet
    Service                   Technology
    Provider                  Training
              Employees
```

with any major facet of your business, it is wise to embrace IT and understand all it can do for your business.

> **QUOTE** *"The way a team plays as a whole determines its success. You may have the greatest bunch of individual stars in the world, but if they don't play together, the club won't be worth a dime." – Babe Ruth*

Many successful small business owners begin their foray into IT by identifying resources, outside their business, to discuss IT needs and direction. Who you talk to and seek advice from is a critical decision. You need to recruit team players – players who will be on your team long-term. Who do you want, and need, on your team? What qualifications should you be looking for? Do you need just a little, or a lot, of help? Let's look at the various classifications of people who may complement and become valuable contributors to the team you intend to build.

> ⭐ TIP Always look for people with experience in both IT AND small business.

Outside Helpers and Contributors

The following classifications are best defined as potential helpers and contributors to your IT team. Generally, they are not suited to setting the overall IT direction and making the necessary long-term planning decisions for your IT needs, unless they also possess detailed skills in both IT and small business.

"**Corporate IT Employee**" – He/she is accustomed to working in an enterprise IT environment which is about as foreign to your needs as imaginable. You have no need for "*multiple domain controllers running redundant pipes to the Internet while maintaining 100% fault tolerance during auto-archive operations.*" The Corporate IT Employee may well play a valuable role in the "desktop" aspects of your software needs, such as Windows XP, Microsoft Office and Outlook.

"**Brother-in-law**" – Your brother-in-law, or any relative not well versed in the field of both IT and small business, is most likely *not* the best person to be providing IT strategy. They may, however, provide valuable assistance in focused areas, such as application software, performing minor PC repairs, etc.

"Current Employee" – The employee who seems to have a basic IT grasp, with no formal training or experience, can actually be an IT planning detriment. Just because the employee understands basic IT procedures and how to rectify certain issues, doesn't make him/her the right person to set the direction for your IT plan. However, they will probably be invaluable to you as a key player in implementation and follow up for your IT needs.

"***College Student***" – College students rarely have the necessary real world or practical experience to evaluate IT strategy beyond technical issues. They may, however, provide a low-cost solution for web page design or quick PC repair when appropriate.

"***Mail Order/Online***" – The catalog or online mail order resource may seem to offer suitable equipment for your small business needs. Generally there is no support for installation questions, configuration concerns, interoperability, etc.

If the decision is made to purchase equipment in this way, bear in mind that your recourse in the event of an incorrect decision is limited, perhaps non-existent. Their "on-site" warranty is usually limited to hardware replacement, not actual restoration of job functions. See Page 102 - the "Pegasus International" case study for an example of mail order warranty service when it is applied in the real world.

"***Project Team***" – This is usually a practical solution for a business owner who has decided to concentrate on a single IT need and solution for that particular problem. For example, a disaster recovery plan or vertical market implementation might require a team of experts to rally around the business and solve it.

Unfortunately, for the small business owner, these decisions are often made without benefit of a cost/benefit analysis first. Owners need to have a firm understanding of the total cost for the team of experts. A Project Team sounds, and frequently is, expensive. While this style of implementation may be a solution for a single project with deep pockets, small business owners rarely have unlimited funds. Frequently, a Project Team is a hybrid of the "College Student" model, described above, with managerial oversight, not always aligned with small business needs. It is critical that your business requirements and resources, as well as a fixed budget, are clearly defined if a Project Team is hired.

"**Computer SuperStore**" – National chain stores, e.g., CompUSA, generally do not possess staff with the required skills to help the small business owner develop a cohesive IT plan. They are, naturally, more focused in selling their products to the consumer market of their business. The store may, however, serve as a reliable resource once you have a firm understanding of equipment needed. These stores are also invaluable when you need a device or a product immediately – such as a network card, a USB hub, etc.

Certain stores also have repair centers located on premises that are available for carry-in work. You will find some that will also service computer notebook equipment as well that eliminates the need to ship a notebook back to the manufacturer for repair.

Outside Vendors

The next classification to consider when assembling your IT team is the "outside vendor." They are personnel, not employed by your small business, who may serve as extremely valuable resources in aiding with IT planning, concepts, and services.

"**Local IT Firm**" – This is the preferred and safest outside vendor to utilize for small business IT needs. Local Firms tend to cover all IT basics, often including phone and on-site support. Ask the right questions when investigating local firms. Investigate the firm's reputation and verify that they've been "around the block" and in business for a number of years. Ask for at least three references and call them! Be sure that rates are in line with industry standards by comparing with a few other IT firms in the area. If they offer an emergency response option, understand the details in the event that you ever need them in a hurry.

"**Local Store**" – A locally owned retail store with on-site service is generally a good small business resource. As with the local IT Firm, determine that they are reputable and have a proven track record. Ask for references and call them as well. Compare rates with the industry standards.

"**Local Accounting Firm**" – Many accounting firms have recently begun to offer "Disaster Planning," "IT consulting," and "Security Overviews." The firm's area of expertise in IT frequently doesn't match the needs of a small business. As with all other outside vendors, it is imperative that references, pricing, and experience with prior small business projects be investigated. Some firms with small business background specializing in "small business technology" are equipped and committed to doing a great job for your company.

Later in this chapter, these classifications are broken down more specifically to help you identify the best questions to ask.

"***Vertical Market Software Vendor***" – These are vendors who sell an entire package, including software, hardware and support for your business. There are literally thousands of them in the marketplace, all with different packages, pricing and track records. Some are great, while others aren't. Some are expensive, others are very reasonable. A solid tip is to bring together either the local IT or local store vendor person to listen to the software vendor presentation. Agree on a consulting fee, if applicable, in advance and bring all the potential players to the table for discussion and planning. Many local IT vendors will participate, at no charge, recognizing the potential for a new customer.

"**Internet Service Provider (ISP)**" – This player will almost certainly be a valuable and necessary component for your IT team. The ISP will provide Internet access for your office. Look for a provider that supplies the highest bandwidth at the lowest cost with the greatest reliability and uptime. In today's market, broadband cable is the best bandwidth for the value. However, if you have specific needs, such as linking multiple offices and networking them across the Internet (or dedicated), you should look for a local company providing service as well as support. The Internet itself is very reliable. Unfortunately, it is not uncommon for the equipment that gets your business on the Internet to malfunction or fail. Quality ISP support will get you back up and running.

"**Web Design Firm**" – You may need to engage a Web Design Firm to create a company presence on the Internet. Read the "The Internet – Your business online" chapter for more detail.

"**Technology Training Centers**" – It is often beneficial to send select employees to outside training classes to lessen the IT learning curve delays and frustrations. There are local training centers throughout the country that offer single day and multi-day IT courses. See the "Putting IT Together" chapter for more training and skill set detail.

"**Off-site Storage Company**" – While this service is usually not available on a small business budget, it is becoming increasingly affordable. It is particularly worth consideration for the small business actively pursuing Disaster Recovery (DR) strategies and business continuity.

Ideally, your IT team will include involvement from a few of the different groups detailed above. As the small business owner, you will need to evaluate the value of each participant, in terms of their knowledge of your "world" and their track record in their own (by calling their references). Consider this a long-term relationship and be committed to investing the proper time and energy to the project. By treating it more like a partnership than a minor task to be crossed off the "to do" list, you will be preparing your small business for success and growth.

What to Look for in Local IT Services

There are many local IT companies available to work with you. Chances are you have already used one or more in your business to fix a problem or install new software and hardware. When discussing who's on your team, however, you'll need a specific set of questions and criteria before forging a long-term relationship with any IT company. A small business may have occasion to use multiple companies from time to time. Whenever possible, keep the services provided by each focused on specific and defined areas.

The following questions will provide a benchmark for you to compare companies:

- Do their references speak highly of them?
- Does the company employ multiple technicians?
- What type of industry certifications does the company itself maintain? (Certified Partner, Gold Partner, etc.)
- What type of industry certifications (see "Common Technician Certifications" section) have their technicians achieved?
- Do they have a helpdesk that allows you to call in and log problems, react to issues and provide immediate resolution when possible?
- Does the company assign a particular technician and/or customer service representative to your company?
- Do they offer emergency response in the event of a system failure?
- Do they offer off-site monitoring of your network, servers and backup status?
- Do they apply periodic updates to your critical servers and operating systems?
- Do they have record keeping in place to accurately track visits to your company, what was done, when, etc.?

- Do they remain current with technology to better provide you with improvement recommendations?
- Are they mindful of your monetary constraints and your budget?
- Have they been in business for a long period of time (at least five years)?
- Do they possess marketing material that backs up their claims with testimonials and certifications?
- Is their main business focus on small businesses?

Common Technician Certifications

In order to gain certification in any area, a technician must pass rigorous tests. Most of them are adaptive in nature, meaning that if an error is made on the test, it adapts by asking more questions in the same area. Certain certifications are a single test; others such as the MCSE certification are six to seven separate tests. While the "passing" levels may vary, suffice it to say that anyone who has passed these tests has mastered the material.

MCP	**M**icrosoft **C**ertified **P**rofessional – has achieved a knowledge of Microsoft Products and operating systems
MCSA	**M**icrosoft **C**ertified **S**ystems **A**dministrator – Has MCP and knowledge of Network Administration
MCSE	**M**icrosoft **C**ertified **S**ystems **E**ngineer – Has MCP, the skills of an MCSA and specializations in particular Microsoft Enterprise products and Network infrastructures
A+	Comptia Certification in Hardware Troubleshooting
Network+	Comptia Certification in General Network Activities
Security+	Comptia Certification in Security Issues and Implementation Strategies
CNA	**N**ovell **C**ertified **N**etware **A**dministrator – Has knowledge of Netware Administration
CNE	**N**ovell **C**ertified **N**etware **E**ngineer – Has CNA and extensive knowledge of Novell products and operating systems
CCNA	**C**isco **C**ertified **N**etwork **A**ssociate – Certified by Cisco Systems in the Basics of networking, including implementation
CCNP	**C**isco **C**ertified **N**etwork **P**rofessional – Certified by Cisco Systems for Local and Wide area networks, including VPN and other broadband technologies
CLE	**C**ertified **L**inux **E**ngineer – Certified by Novell in the details of the Linux operating system

There are other higher level certifications available. However any that exceed the above skill sets are usually too expensive for small business needs and don't make a good fit when shopping for IT professionals in your market. These credentials can be easily verified by requesting confirmation from each company offering the certification.

Who Else is on My Team?

Looking outside your business for sound advice and direction is a prudent course of action. However, there are people within your organization currently that will add unique talents to the team as well. Some of the individuals may have been listed among the types that would not be good "planners," but they will most likely be excellent additions to the team when it comes to implementing an IT concept or direction.

Employees

The small business Office Manager or Bookkeeper should be on the IT team. They play a vital role in your business by keeping the administrative side of your business flowing. They may be particularly valuable in using their organizational skills for backup management, software organization, and process-related issues. Generally, the skill set of the office manager or bookkeeper doesn't equip them to be the leader of the IT team. Also, if they were successful in this role, it could create a very risky position you, the small business owner, giving them too much control. In the worst case scenario, if they fail, you may be out of business!

The Plant Manager or Operations Supervisor in a manufacturing small business should also be on the IT team, serving as the front line of communication with workers when something goes wrong. If you have a current employee who has assumed some (or the entire) IT role, they should also be put on the team.

Owner

The small business owner is the most critical team player! IT is so pervasive in any business that it can't be treated lightly or as an afterthought to be delegated to someone else. You must understand the concepts, equipment and methods used in the IT world and, just as importantly, understand how they impact daily operations of your business.

> ⓘ RULE **YOU, the business owner, are the most important player on the IT team.**

What Does IT Cost?

One of the biggest areas of concern in the small business arena is always cost, but this is especially true of the IT cost. Larger businesses prepare annual budgets to forecast what they will need to allocate for IT expenses. A small business, as a rule, doesn't take the time to plan at that level. Usually, expenditures are quick, unplanned reactions to a crisis or a failed piece of equipment. However, even an extremely busy small business owner can use some of the information contained in this chapter to get a handle on the type of spending required to properly address IT needs.

In the financial planning world, a common budget figure to use for IT maintenance alone would be ½ to 1% of total annual sales. For example, if annual sales are $750,000, expect IT maintenance costs ranging from $3250 to $7500 annually. This does not include capital purchases, such as computers and other hardware. It is simply the expected maintenance amount that will probably be necessary for service calls, labor for upgrades and installations, phone support, etc. There are other recurring fixed costs such as Internet access and web hosting that most accountants categorize as general office expenses. These are also not included in the maintenance costs.

> QUOTE "The bitterness of **poor quality** remains long after the sweetness of the **low price** is forgotten." - *Anonymous*

If you wish to get a more precise, all inclusive total, the example below would be a good start. This example assumes that you have 10 employees in your company who utilize some form of IT. Shared costs, such as file servers and network resources, are divided by the number of users who use the resource. Other products, such as software, are usually divided among the entire employee population, as the internal systems should benefit everyone in the company.

Annual Cost Calculations

Use the worksheet below to determine the CPUA – The **C**ost **p**er **U**ser **A**nnually. This number tends to be fairly constant over time based on the average employee count. This number can be extremely helpful when planning for future growth of your company and the expected increased costs, therein.

IT – Budget Worksheet

Category	Cost	# of Users	Life	CPUA*
Hardware				
Computer	1000	1	4	250
Server	6000	10	5	120
Network Communication Equipment	1000	10	5	20
Network Cabling	1500	10	10	15
Printers	800	10	3	26
Software				
Anti-Virus Subscription	50	1	1	50
Accounting Software	500	10	5	50
MS Office Basic	250	1	3	83
Vertical App 1	7000	10	5	140
Vertical App Annual	1400	10	1	140
Internet Costs				
Broadband Connection	1200	10	1	120
Web Hosting Fees	200	10	1	20
Domain Name Registration	50	10	1	5
Support Costs				
External Maintenance	4200	10	1	420
Floor Space/Utilities	3600	10	1	360
Internal Support	7500	10	1	750

PC Helpdesk Subscription	200	10	1	20
Consumables				
Paper	500	10	1	50
Toner and Ink	800	10	1	80
Backup Media	250	10	1	25
CDs/DVDs	200	10	1	20
*** **Totals:**				**2764**

* CPUA – Cost per user annually

In order to calculate the per user cost, take the cost of a line item and divide by the number of benefiting users. Then, divide by the number of useful service years expected from the line item. This results in the Cost per User Annually.

As you can see from the worksheet, one of the highest costs is internal support. This is the cost of your employees' involvement in the inner workings of IT. For instance, when you have a printer jam, there is usually an employee who comes and fixes it. If a user has a problem with a Word document or a spreadsheet, an employee generally corrects it. All of these related events have an "opportunity cost" associated with them. That is, the employee spending time on IT functions cannot be productive in other business roles. You, as the owner, need to be very careful of the amount of time spent in this regard. It can consume substantial amounts of employee time that you may not have planned for this role and function.

> ⚠ CAUTION *The employee who is spending time supporting IT issues cannot be productive in other roles that you may have assigned.*

In order to keep this cost as low as possible, consider subscribing to a helpdesk service. It is also possible that your IT resource will provide this support at an additional cost. In any case, you will usually find it to be much more cost effective than using your internal staff to provide this support.

Total Cost of Ownership

Another method of calculating costs over time is Total Cost of Ownership (TCO). This method was created by the Gartner Group, an IT research firm, in 1987. It created quite a stir when first formulated, because it demonstrated that a single PC purchase could result in a $10,000 total cost. It has, over the years, become an accepted forecasting method for larger companies.

It is easy to understand the TCO concept when applied to the automobile industry, where it is commonly used. To calculate the TCO of an automobile, add together the purchase price, all maintenance, repair and gasoline purchases, driver training, upgrades, final disposition, and advertising costs for resale, etc. A variant of this total is to use it at an annual level. Assume in the same example, that the automobile will be used for five years. Simply divide the TCO by five to get the annual cost.

The TCO and CPUA methods provide a more accurate cost estimate than simply comparing the Total Cost of Acquisition (TCA). Take the time to construct a working spreadsheet of the above items and insert your costs. It will be immediately apparent that there is more to consider than simply the initial purchase price.

What TCO and CPUA don't consider are the long-term **benefits** of competing products. They only calculate the long-term **cost** of an item. The small business owner still needs to factor in and compare every IT purchase for its Return on Investment (ROI) value to the business.

Return on Investment

Though this book is not a financially oriented resource, most will agree that, while Return on Investment (ROI) is extremely important to all businesses, it is especially critical to the small business where cash flow is usually much tighter.

Therefore, each new IT acquisition should be weighed in terms of direct cost/benefit to the company. Consider the following:

- Does the purchase "protect the business" with improved equipment?

- Does the purchase have a direct revenue generating effect?

- Does the purchase increase productivity in such a way that the purchase will pay for itself over its expected life?

- Does the purchase lessen the complexity of overall IT within the company?

- Is the purchase a proven tool or an unproven gadget?

The 10 Most Critical IT Pitfalls

If you only walk away with a handful of ideas from this book, the following list highlights important issues to discuss with your IT team. If you don't take steps to protect your business from these pitfalls, you will eventually pay. How much? This can vary greatly depending on the problem, and can range from unproductive man hours, lost customer revenue, damaged business reputation, and even, in extreme situations, a failed business. As the owner of a small business, you don't want to waste even a minute of your valuable time figuring out how to recover from **avoidable** pitfalls.

The 10 Pitfalls

Pitfall	Covered
Not making a valid data backup on a daily basis	Page 100
Performing software upgrades without a proven, tested backup	Page 41
Not having off-site storage of your data	Page 101
Not having on-site and off-site storage of application software, operating system disks, and printouts of equipment configurations	Page 69
Assuming that someone else is "on top" of these issues and carefully monitoring them to verify they are done	Page 30
Running "critical" computers without Uninterruptible Power Supplies and up-to-date virus protection	Page 120
Allowing access to both your network resources and application software with little or no password security	Page 74
Unblocked access into and out of your	Page 60

company via the Internet	
↓ Lack of e-mail SPAM protection and spyware filters	Page 92
↓ Allowing employees complete access to servers and internal systems via telecommuting	Page 74

The common theme surrounding each pitfall is the focus on protecting your business. Small business owners understand the need to focus all decisions and strategies on the imperative rule of protecting their investment and future.

> (i) **RULE** **Protect your Business!**

The following case study provides an example of what can happen when only a handful of these mistakes are made.

> **Case Study: Northwest Grinding Corporation**
>
> A small manufacturing firm was using vertical market software to control their shop floor. They were using Peachtree software for their accounting. All of this data was properly located on a central file server running Windows 2000 with a software mirror. They had received detailed instructions on how to check their tape backups daily, as well as instructions on proper tape rotation.
>
> Months later, they received a "mirror failure" message. Not knowing what it meant, they clicked on the "OK" button and the message disappeared. They wrongly assumed that the problem had been corrected. To compound matters, they quickly tired of rotating the tapes daily, so they simply left one tape in the drive and allowed it to overwrite itself on a nightly basis.
>
> One year later, they called their service company because no one in the office could connect to the server. The technician arrived and a high-pitched whine was emitting from the server. There was a blank monitor screen as well. "Wow," the technician said as he reviewed the server configuration, "be thankful that you have a mirrored drive in here." He disconnected the faulty

drive and configured the server to boot from the mirror. The words on the screen were "Boot Device Failure." No one had ever called the support company about the "mirror failure" error message first observed a year before.

He replaced one faulty drive with a new one and asked for the client's original operating system CD's. The client had no idea what and where these could be. He loaded a temporary copy of the operating system and then asked for their backup tapes. They explained their "new" way of backing up their data and, as he ejected their only backup tape, dust spewed out and clung to the media. When the tape was re-inserted, it was unreadable. They had no other backups anywhere.

Every bit of business data was lost forever. (An attempt was made to use a data recovery service. It also failed.)

Protect Your Business

Keep Up with Current Technology - Carefully

There are many facets to consider in the IT world. You must stay current enough with technology to not lose pace, yet recognize that change can be very disruptive. You need to keep key employees challenged and made to feel that the company is committed to technology and continual improvement, but not at the expense of exposing the business unnecessarily.

As you read this book, you'll begin to get an overall sense for what your IT direction and needs should be. Naturally, this varies from business to business. There is no right and wrong way when setting IT direction. There are too many factors, e.g., budget, employee skill sets, physical assets in use, etc. There are, however, many right procedures to follow and wrong turns to avoid!

In the continuing quest to protect a small business, owners need to weigh expense and exposure versus downtime at all times. There are situations when spending money to stay current with technology is money well spent.

> **Case Study: Johnson Fastener Corporation**
>
> The Johnson Fastener Corporation has been in business since 1947. The firm was founded by Mr. Johnson and has grown into a multimillion dollar company, employing more than 160 people. It is still a family business.
>
> They always invested in new technology. In the mid 1970's, they adopted Wang word processing for their correspondence and quoting systems. When the mini-computer became a viable option a few years later, they invested heavily in automating their shop floor. When Mr. Johnson's son entered management, they spent large amounts on the, then unknown, concept of "just in time" warehousing and production. When the PC became mainstream in the late 1980's, they converted. In the early to mid 1990's, they rewrote their shop floor management system and implemented several interfaces that Mr. Johnson's son had personally developed using cutting edge technology. And then,

> when the basic business needs were met, they stopped further software development and upgrades.
>
> Now, fast forward to 2006. They are still running those PC systems from the 1980's and fine tuned in the 1990's. They have a few consultants to apply patches and attempt to keep everything running. However, it is becoming difficult to acquire PC hardware technology for decades-old software. They are also faced with problems using the data contained in the old systems - making it available to their customers, Internet issues, etc.
>
> The company is faced with a major decision. Do they begin the development cycle again, building new internal systems to take advantage of today's technology? Do they commit to an MRP solution costing hundreds of thousands to millions to implement?

This demonstrates the position that you don't want to find yourself in when it comes to technology. If the Johnson Company commits to new software now, they are faced with huge development and purchase expenditures. There will be thousands of man-hours consumed in the training and implementation of a new system that virtually becomes a new way of doing any daily job function, from reading of a factory order all the way to shipping the finished product. The real cost is the human cost of fixing this problem - all of the hours that are entailed that will not provide truly productive time to the company's bottom line.

Their only long-term solution is to embrace a vertical market package from a reputable company, borrow money to float the payments over the next decade, provide on-site trainers, and demonstrate a commitment to spend whatever is necessary to implement the new system.

The Johnson Company should have continued their own in-house development cycle onto new platforms, as they had been doing. They would have been in a position to gradually accept new software and solutions into their business model. The hours spent in implementing change would have been over a long period of time and would greatly lessen the human cost.

Implement Application Software Upgrades with Care

Application software upgrades are a double-edged sword. On one hand, as demonstrated with the Johnson Company, keeping pace with technological advances is necessary and increases productivity and morale. On the other hand, software upgrades may corrupt data or cause other costly business interruptions. In some instances, it doesn't make a lot of business sense.

> ★TIP Wait at least 90 days from receipt of a new application software upgrade before applying it. You never want to be the "first on the block" to experience problems with upgrades.

One of the deciding upgrade factors is a software vendor's "end-of-life" statement (usually found on the vendor web site). Generally, if a vendor is planning to, or has recently, dropped support for a given software product, most often in favor of a new version or release, it is wise to upgrade to that version. As a general rule, you don't want to be using software in the daily operation of your business that is no longer supported. The exception is when your business wouldn't even notice if a problem developed in the application or in the data.

When evaluating whether to perform a software upgrade, use the following checklist to determine the risk of exposure to potential problems:

Software Upgrade Checklist

- ☐ Is the vendor terminating support for the current version that you are using?
- ☐ Are the new features in the release update listed in such a way that you can adequately evaluate their usefulness?
- ☐ If so, are they features that will help productivity substantially?
- ☐ Does any data need to be manually entered to use this release?
- ☐ Does this release require operating system "patches" to be applied?

- ☐ Does this release require updates to printer drivers?
- ☐ Does this release require any changes externally for Internet access, etc.?
- ☐ Is there extensive downtime involved with performing the upgrade?
- ☐ Can you accurately make a complete valid backup just prior to the upgrade in the event of a "fall back?"
- ☐ Is the software vendor available via phone and/or remote connection if the need arises to "fall back" to an earlier version?

You should know the answers to these questions **prior** to making a decision to install any upgrades. Every checklist question is vitally important because, if there is a failure on any point, it may have adverse ramifications for your business.

Down Time Calculator:
Application Failure: Lost Hours * Overhead Cost per Employee * # of Users
Example: (8 hours * $25.00) * 10 = **$2,000 lost production for eight Down Time Hours**

Educate Your Employees About Your IT Policy

It can be difficult to explain the critical need for data privacy and security measures to employees, especially when the business owner may not completely understand the issues. Too often, when things are operating properly, the measures and rules may seem unnecessarily strict and prohibitive.

Unfortunately, when an employee performs a simple task such as opening a personal e-mail attachment, the entire company can be exposed to possible harm. This awareness needs to be emphasized to all employees, so that they realize the possible ramifications of their basic actions.

Communicating simple rules to all employees will eliminate some of the risks. You, as the business owner, wear many, many hats. Now it's time to put on your Human Resources hat and educate your employees. Usually, this is done in the form of a memo sent to all employees and also, if available, the policies should be placed in an employee handbook (or SOP). It is essential that employees understand the rules and your total commitment to their implementation. Consider these rules and modify to include anything specific to your business culture and situation:

- All employees are responsible for protecting the privacy of the business data, including any copying or transfers of data from the premises.

- All employees are responsible for what they do on the Internet during company time.

- All employees are responsible for any personal e-mail received at work that might potentially harm your network. Under no circumstances should employees ever give out their business e-mail address for personal use.

- All employees are responsible for any attachment opened while on the company network.

- All employees are responsible to obey the rules of the company regarding central file storage and organization. They will do their best to store documents in the proper location.

- All employees are responsible for keeping their passwords private. Passwords should never be taped to monitors or written on sticky notes. Instead, create a file folder of this information to be tucked away.

- All employees are responsible for verifying that their virus software is current on their office PC.

- The designated employee is responsible for validating and rotating the backup media used in the company.

- The designated employee is responsible for knowing what software has been updated, and for keeping the official off-site copies up-to-date.

> ⚠ **CAUTION** A Salary.com/AOL poll (July 2005) estimated that the average employee wastes more than two hours each day at work. Topping the list as wasteful activities were personal e-mail correspondence and web surfing.

However, responsibility for all of the items listed above ultimately rests on the shoulders of the company and the owner. You are responsible to verify that these guidelines are being adhered to and it is your oversight that will make them actual company policy.

Employee Training

As a business owner, you appreciate the value of a trained, competent employee. Most small businesses provide "on the job" employee training. However, there are certain IT skills so intrinsic to every job function that either the new hire must demonstrate proficiency during the interview phase, or training must be provided immediately. Never underestimate the value of an employee already skilled in various IT disciplines. One of the important building blocks for successful IT implementation will involve a planned employee training schedule.

> 💬 **QUOTE** *"The great aim of education is not knowledge but action." - Herbert Spencer*

In 1976, John Nevison coined the term "computer literacy." He recognized that future workers would need to be well-rounded in information skills and the use of computerization. Thirty years later, "computer literate" has evolved to define an individual who is not only comfortable around computers, but one who can easily use

44

them for business and personal advancement that contributes to an overall benefit to themselves.

Local IT Training Venues

Many local IT training companies offer free, small audience, one-to three-hour sessions on various topics. These companies offer seminars to entice business owners and employees, hoping they will realize the value of additional training. Take advantage of these no-cost opportunities as they present themselves. Better yet, call a few of your local IT training companies and ask to be added to their e-mail distribution list. You, and your employees, can gain invaluable FREE knowledge and experience by attending!

Before you can even attempt to approach education, however, you will need to know exactly what you and your employees know and don't know. The following section will help you ascertain just what, where and who will need additional "basic training" for your IT business needs.

Skill Set Profile

The following skill set profile can be used as a guideline for every employee working with a PC. Without these skills, and the opportunity to develop new skills, technology will eventually surpass the employee, making them inadequate and making their performance ineffective. Equipping all employees with these skills will provide higher employee and customer satisfaction, not to mention saving the business money and adding efficiency. The profile can be used to evaluate existing staff and as a hiring tool.

IT Skill Assessment Profile

The Essentials:

↓ Keyboarding/Typing Skills	
↓ Basic Mouse Skills	

The Basics:

↓ Windows XP Operating System	
o How to Sign On	
o How to Start a Program	
o Windows Explorer	
o How to Search for a File	
↓ Basic Application Software	
o Microsoft WordPad	
o Microsoft Word	
o Microsoft Excel	
↓ Basic Internet Software	
o E-mail (Microsoft Outlook, Microsoft Outlook Express)	
• Compose/Send/Receive	
o Microsoft Internet Explorer	
• Site Navigation	

• Search Engines (Google, MSN, Yahoo)	

Advanced Operations

↓ Creating Shortcuts	
↓ Control Panel Items	
↓ Uninstalling Software	
↓ Microsoft Outlook	
o Address Books/Contacts	
o Exporting/Importing Data	
↓ Virus Updates	
↓ Operating System Software Updates	

Server Based Functions (General)

↓ Add/Remove Users and User Information	
↓ Verify/Confirm Backup Operations via Software	

Review the above profile to evaluate all employees in your company. Place a checkmark next to each line as you identify an employee currently demonstrating that skill. Be certain that you have at least two checkmarks for each function in order to adequately fill the needs of your company. Contact your local IT training center to develop a plan for any skills that don't have two or more checkmarks. This will provide balance and growth opportunities for your business. Your employees will also appreciate the opportunity to become more proficient in new areas.

If your company uses spreadsheets and word processing heavily, be sure to have all employees trained in their use. It helps to have all employees doing things the same way when using these tools.

Application Software

Virtually all small businesses use software, in one form or another, in direct support of their business. This is, in fact, what the term "application software" means. Perhaps you are using Microsoft Excel or Intuit QuickBooks to generate company invoices. You may be using Microsoft Word or Quoteworks to generate customer quotes. All of these are examples of application software packages.

It's possible that you are already utilizing a vertical-market application, an application tailored specifically for your business or industry. These are generally quite expensive to purchase and implement, but because they provide a more customized fit, in general, they are chosen when available. Many owners rightly choose not to re-invent the wheel if a vertical-market application is available.

Application software can add efficiency to your business when understood and used properly. When poorly understood and implemented, it may negatively impact your business. As the business owner, your understanding of how the software is being used, who is using it, and what it is, or is not, doing for your business is crucial.

Often, there are internal systems within a small business, built around the use of software applications. For instance, you may be using Microsoft Excel to produce invoices. The invoices may then be used as the packing slip and/or pick ticket. As internal processes are reviewed and evaluated, familiarity and customized practices should also be weighed in terms of change, efficiency, etc.

> **⭐ TIP** *If your business runs via a number of disjointed forms, incompatible software applications and internal systems, consider purchasing an all-inclusive software product, specific to your business or industry.*

It is also very important to weigh your company's future goals and direction when selecting application software. The decision needs to result in growth opportunities and technology advancements. Usually, there are a number of viable vertical market packages, although they can be very expensive to purchase and implement.

If you do not currently utilize a vertical market application in your business, it can be very beneficial to periodically test the waters to see what is available on the market. This is especially true if your current systems aren't working properly and tend to be "bandaged" together.

Some specific examples of vertical market applications include:

Construction	**Shop Floor**	**Dental**
Expedition	Shop Boss	Soft Dent
Estimator	DCD	Eagle Soft
Accounting	**Law Firms**	Dentrix
Account Mate	Timeslips	**Taxation**
PeachTree	PC Law	LaCerte

Where to look for vertical market software:

- The Internet
- Trade Magazines/Publications
- Networking Groups/References

How to evaluate vertical market software:

What? – What job functions in your company does this software need to perform?

Why? – Why would you choose this particular piece of software? Does it have the best "features list?"

How? – How easy is it to use? Will it provide meaningful data easily? Does it interface well with the Internet and other software, such as Microsoft Office, etc.?

Who? – Who will use it? Is the software company reputable?

When? – When can it be installed? How long will it take to implement?

Cost? – What does it cost to purchase? What are the annual maintenance fees? What are the training costs?

Trial Software

Perhaps one of the best features of the Internet is the ability to download software. There are many vertical market software packages available for free download. Even if you decide that it doesn't meet your specific needs, invariably they will demonstrate new business approaches and ideas.

> **TIP** *"When I was evaluating software for the TAB helpdesk, I downloaded and reviewed seven software packages over a three-month period. Next, I made a "features list" for each and compared them. While I ended up enhancing the system we already had in place, it was a fantastic process to collect some new ideas and approaches for a specific software application."* T.J.

Online Demonstrations

Many software vendors now offer online/real-time software demonstrations directly from the Internet. This is another strategy to develop criteria for your "features list" and to actually identify the most suitable software package available.

Demonstration CD's

Demonstration CDs can be another great way to evaluate software. Many times, demonstration CDs are also fully functioning programs that allow you to accurately measure the software as it relates directly to your company. Demonstration CDs are, sometimes, a simple slide show which doesn't necessarily help significantly in evaluation.

Shareware Software

Amazingly, there are thousands of vertical market applications available as shareware. Shareware is the ultimate "try before you buy" software solution. Try out http://www.shareware.com and see what you can find! These are also a great idea source to better understand your software needs.

As the following case study illustrates, it pays to do your homework and take time in planning new software implementations.

Cape Cod Eye Associates

Cape Cod Eye Associates had been using a billing system that was very appropriate for their needs through the end of the 1990's. When the Year 2000 programming issues arose, the vendor responded admirably to the hysteria and provided a very good comfort zone for the office staff. The year 2000 came and went and their billing system still worked.

The partners in the practice wanted to continue to use the existing vendor, but, unfortunately, the new software that

> the vendor had introduced was very expensive. The vendor was also dropping all support for their current "DOS" based software. So, they went shopping for a new package.
>
> They reviewed a number of packages and narrowed to three choices they thought might work. Two, they thought, would work well and only one they felt had the growth potential with new modules, paperless office, etc. The package they decided on was 1/3 the cost of the others - a huge selling point.
>
> They were provided a number of online sessions to see how the new software worked. They requested and received a detailed requirements list for hardware and software configurations from the vendor. In addition, they asked the software vendor for a list of consultants in their area who were familiar with the implementation of their software package. They interviewed the consultants via phone and selected the individual who specialized in optometric practices.
>
> Once provided with hardware specifications, they solicited bids from two local hardware vendors. They made the decision to avoid the "mail order" business – they needed reassurance that help would be available when they needed it. For the price difference, it simply was not worth the risk to them.
>
> They selected a hardware vendor based on both price and reputation and placed that vendor in touch with their software consultant. Together, they finalized what exactly was needed for the practice and a final hardware/software plan and implementation list was created.
>
> The implementation was performed over a weekend with great success. The data conversion from the old system did not go as planned, but the office staff was able to recreate the records in the new system over a two-month period to recover. The software company credited the conversion costs.

This process is about as "textbook" as one can get to achieving the perfect implementation of a new software package. It's an example that all professionals should read before attempting.

Your IT Team

Now that you have a complete feel for what possible players are involved for your team, it's time to assign responsibilities to the people in your organization. Be certain to sit with each person on the list to explain the required tasks and responsibilities. Use this book as a guide and have them read the applicable section(s). Be absolutely confident that everyone understands their role and tasks.

If you are using outside vendors, write a small description of the tasks they will be responsible for and e-mail or fax it to them. As with your employees, they are part of your IT team and they should be crystal clear in what results are expected.

IT Team Worksheet

Category	Responsible Person
Technology Oversight	You
Budget/Acquisition of IT Items	
PC Support and Maintenance	
Web Site Hosting	
Internet Support	
File Server Maintenance	
Backup – Daily	
Backup - Off-site Storage	
Budget Planning – Upgrades	
Company Software – Copies	
Company Software – Off-site Storage	
Administrator's Handbook	
Employee IT Training	
HelpDesk / Problem resolution	

The next chapter will focus on these tasks in more detail, and prepare you to properly evaluate the necessary steps to safeguard your IT organizational plan.

Get IT Organized!!

Introduction

This chapter focuses on the often overlooked, but so critical, organizational component in the IT world. Users often wrongly assume that the computer "will keep them organized." Nothing, in fact, could be further from the truth! Without an organized IT approach, disorganization, lost data, and most importantly, loss of IT control are not far behind. Let's examine each area requiring a logical and organized approach to achieve success.

> **QUOTE** *Organizing is what you do before you do something, so that when you do it, it is not all mixed up. – A.A. Milne*

Administrator's Handbook

Begin the process with a two-inch, three-ring binder and page dividers. This handbook will contain essential information about your IT world, all organized in a single resource. It is imperative that the handbook be reviewed and updated regularly. Outlined below, are the essential sections to build your "weapon of organization."

	Emergency Contact List
	User Profile Sheets
	Router/Gateway/ISP Information Sheet
	File Server Folder Structure
	Asset listing of IT Equipment in Use
	Digital Camera Photos
	Software Organization and Storage

You may need to purchase a few items that will greatly facilitate your overall organization. Consider them a worthwhile investment!

Purchase a "Dymo™" label printer (approximately $30 at any Office SuperStore). Throughout the book, there will be label-making instructions. The Dymo™ label printer seems to work best in terms of equipment adherence.

Purchase an inexpensive lock box to store your on-site tapes. The box should be small enough to locate next to, or near, your file server. Use the box to store the tapes when they are not being used in the server. Never leave active backup tapes lying on desks or the floor unprotected. In the instances when your backup becomes necessary, this might be your only chance to retrieve data.

Another reason to store backup tapes out of easy reach is because of their sensitive content. Backup tapes will contain ALL important and sensitive company information. If the data is not encrypted during the backup, and most aren't, or the tape set doesn't require a password, a misplaced tape is just minutes away from being stolen and restored outside of your company. At that point, your business is totally exposed. In addition, if your business is liable under governmental regulations such as HIPAA, Sarbanes-Oxley, SEC Rule 17a-4 or GLBA, there would be fines and/or prison time for this "oversight."

Emergency Contact List

The first page of your administrator handbook should contain a list of critical people, and their contact information, to be readily available when needed quickly. Make certain to include the following:

- Key Employees
- Software Vendors

- Contractor Vendors
    - Heating/Air Conditioning
    - Plumbing
    - Electrician
    - IT Service Provider
    - Internet Service Provider

Include as much information as possible, such as hours of operation, pager numbers, home phones, helpdesk/support numbers, etc. In short, include any and all possible means of getting in touch with these key players when the need arises.

> **⚠ CAUTION** *Make certain a copy of this entire handbook is kept off-site.*

User Profile Sheet

Each employee using a PC in your organization should have a user profile sheet. This single piece of paper should contain basic information to be utilized in the event of a system problem. Some information may be specific to the user's software as well. Always include:

User Name:	
Password:	Remote Access? Yes No
E-Mail Address:	IM? ☐ AOL ☐ MS ☐ Yahoo
E-Mail Client:	Screen Name:
My Documents Folder:	Application – SignOn Info
Applications Used:	
User Specific Notes:	

Narrative:

User Name	A generally accepted standard for a user name is comprised of the first initial of first name, optionally a middle initial if a duplicate name would be created, and a full spelling of the last name. Example: John S. Smith and John J. Smith would be jssmith and jjsmith respectively. If a duplicate would not be created, first initial, last name is fine, i.e., bmiller
Password	There are many opinions about what constitutes a "good" password. There is a section of this book that discusses passwords and their implementation. There are a number of products that can "crack" a password in a matter of seconds. Any combination of at least seven numbers and special characters makes it significantly more difficult to crack. Some administrators don't track user passwords, simply allowing users to manage them. This is perfectly acceptable, provided that the administrator has a way to reset passwords when necessary. In the Windows security arena, this is not an issue.
Remote Access	Indicate whether the user has remote access permissions.
E-mail Address	Whenever possible, use one of two standards – username@domain or first.lastname@domain. This is also covered in further detail in this book.
E-mail Client	If you own MS Office, MS Outlook is a good client choice. If not, Outlook Express is distributed with the Windows operating system and also works well. There are many other excellent E-mail clients (Thunderbird, etc.), but business support is generally not available.
IM?	Note any known Instant Messenger Services that the user accesses at work.

Screen Name	Attempt to use the User Name and the Domain Name for the screen name.
MyDocuments Folder	Establish a unique file server folder named "Employee Documents." Establish a sub-folder with the user name of each employee within the folder. This folder should be used in place of any local drive for storing documents. This is discussed in detail in the "file folder" section of the book.
Application Sign-on Info	If you utilize software applications specific to your industry, include sign-on information required to get the user into the system. It's helpful to also indicate security levels, etc., that might need to be reset.
Applications Used	List each application that this user accesses on a regular basis. In the event of a PC replacement and/or planned upgrade, an Inventory of which users use what applications is invaluable.
Specific Notes	Supply any and all information that might be useful to know about this user, especially applicable detail remote access information, etc.

ROUTER/Gateway/ISP Information Sheet

Internet Access/Router Configuration

The easiest way to gather information about your network equipment is to print out (or take print screens of) the current configurations. This configuration information should also be included in your off-site handbook. Without this vital data, valuable time will be lost re-creating the information in event of an equipment failure. The short list below represents the minimum amount of necessary information for your current network environment:

Router Configuration Worksheet

Router Model:	Date:
User Sign On:	Password:
IP Address:	Static or DHCP (circle one)
Gateway IP:	Internal IP Scheme: 192.168.x.x
DNS1	DNS2:
Port Forwarding: IP:	Port Forwarding: IP:
SMTP Host:	POP3 Host:
SMTP Authentication:	POP3 Authentication:
PPPoE User Name:	PPPoE Password:

You may have no idea what all these terms mean at this point, but it is imperative that you have this information available both on-site and off-site in the event of an equipment failure. Your Internet connection may not work properly without this information being available for the technician arriving to remedy the equipment issue.

The sample pictures below illustrate some common models of routers and firewalls (a specific type of router). It is very important that your Internet access be properly configured. The general concept is to allow as little access both into and out from your internal network as possible while still giving you functionality. The configuration information that you have recorded will be how your IT service firm can confirm your level of safety.

TIP *If your Internet router is in a secure location, use a label printer to affix the sign-on name and passwords directly to the device.*

File Server Folder Structure

Volumes can be written about the proper way to organize your server files and folders. The following is an acceptable and commonly used guideline. Names can be customized to more closely match the needs of your organization, but the grouping of data works well for virtually any office.

> (i) **RULE** **Never** store company documents on a local PC.
> **Always** store them where they are globally accessible and safe.

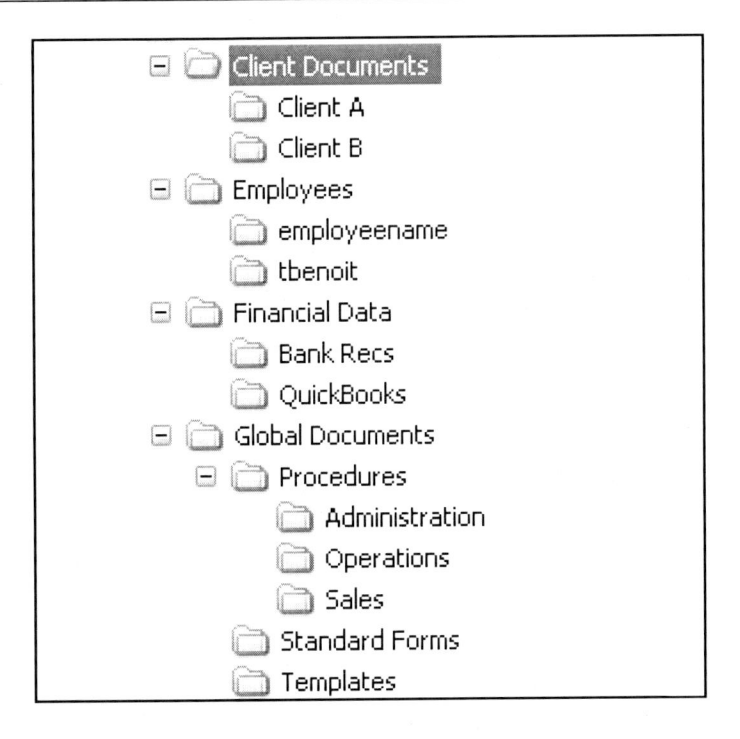

```
□ 📁 Client Documents
    📁 Client A
    📁 Client B
□ 📁 Employees
    📁 employeename
    📁 tbenoit
□ 📁 Financial Data
    📁 Bank Recs
    📁 QuickBooks
□ 📁 Global Documents
    □ 📁 Procedures
        📁 Administration
        📁 Operations
        📁 Sales
    📁 Standard Forms
    📁 Templates
```

A good electronic filing system should mimic an organized paper filing system. Items should be properly labeled and placed in electronic "drawers" with electronic "folders." Folders should contain logical descriptions on the "page" which quickly and accurately identify the sub-folder and file content.

Folder	Sub-Folder
Employees	Each employee should have a unique folder on the file server identified with their user name. This folder should be their "home" folder and should eliminate the common practice of storing files in the "My Documents" folder on the individual PC. Employee-specific files should be stored here.
Global Documents	This folder area is used to store company documents of a global nature. Sub-folders often include: Human Resources, Legal Documents, Graphics (used for letterhead), and Marketing Materials.
Client Documents	Every client document produced should be self contained within this folder, including correspondence to/from the client and pertinent photos and images. It is perfectly acceptable to call this class of information "Customer Data" or something similar. Whatever fits your current description is fine, as long as everyone in your company describes it in the same format.
Financial Data	This folder should be protected from normal view using the security capabilities of your file server. Examples of sub-folders found in this directory include: Accounting System Data, Month End Reports, etc.
Downloaded Software	This folder should contain any software purchased online. In all such instances, a downloadable installation program will place the purchased software on your system. Always order the hard copy CD and manual, if this is an option at time of purchase. As with all software, make a

| | backup copy of the installation program for your Archival Backup Copy (ABC) to be stored off-site. |

File Naming Conventions

File Names in Windows 95 and newer can be up to 255 characters long. They are not "case sensitive" (i.e. meaning Windows treats capitalized and lower case letters alike) and can contain spaces within the file name. The only characters NOT allowed in a file name are \ / : * ? " < > and ¦ . They sometimes act as if they are case sensitive (in name sorts, etc.), but they are not.

> ⭐TIP *Windows file names are not case sensitive.*

They are formatted in <name>.<extension> format (with the dot acting as a spacer between them), but the extension is optional. Strangely, the file name can contain multiple periods as well resulting in some unique file names! An extension, when used, is the manner in which Windows handles "file associations" – the way a file is opened, edited, updated, etc. Windows contains an extensive list of known file extensions, along with the associated programs required to handle them. However, you do have the ability to modify any and all associations in the operating system if necessary.

A recommended approach to creating file names is to only use lower case letters, avoid spaces and use a single '.' in the name, along with a logical extension. For example, a spreadsheet containing fourth quarter financials could be called "financials-qtr4-2006.xls." Remember when using Windows Explorer, you can sort by the file name column. Use this feature to your advantage when creating file names, so that files present in logical groups when viewed.

> **TIP** Be consistent and logical when naming files. Consistency in naming files helps not only you, but others who may be looking for a file tomorrow or a year from now. Utilize the "alphabetic order" feature.

Avoid using acronyms and other abbreviations within file names, unless they are commonly recognized by all employees who might need access. It is imperative that file names make sense to all users.

Unix/Linux/Apple File Names

Because Windows is talking to other operating systems, it's worth pausing to note some key differences between them. First, with all these operating systems, both directory names and file names ARE case sensitive at all levels. For instance, "\internal\test.txt" is not the same location or file name as "\Internal\Test.TXT." In the Windows world, they would be. Some programs that are carried over from the Unix world such as FTP or TELNET often create confusion when used to access Unix/Linux systems for this reason. Be aware of this when using any Interface that is not "speaking" in a Window's language!

Common List of File Extensions

System		Images	
.bak	Backup File	.bmp	Bitmap Image
.dll	Dynamic Link Library	.gif	Compuserve Graphical Interchange
.exe	Executable Program File	.jpg	JPEG File
.sys	System File	.psd	Photoshop Image
MS Office		.tif	Tagged Image File
.doc	Word Document	.wmf	Windows Metafile
.mdb	Access Database	**Audio/Video**	
.ppt	PowerPoint Presentation	.avi	Interleaved Animation
.prj	Project File	.mp3	Compressed Audio
.tmp	Temporary File	.mp4	Compressed Video/Audio
.xls	Excel Workbook	.mpg	MPEG Movie
Internet		.wav	Waveform Audio File
.asp	Active Server Page	**Miscellaneous**	
.cfm	ColdFusion (Adobe)	.pdf	Adobe Portable Document
.htm	Hypertext Markup	.txt	Text File
.swf	Shockwave (Adobe)	.zip	Zipped (Compressed) File
		.bat	Batch Execution Commands
		.qb	QuickBooks Data

Windows will, by default, hide file extensions from view. This can be a problem if you rename a file by accident or misplace a file. In order to turn off this feature, open "My Computer" or "Windows Explorer." Select the "View Menu" and click "Folder Options." Click on the "View" tab to view options. Under "Advanced Settings," uncheck "Hide extensions for known file types."

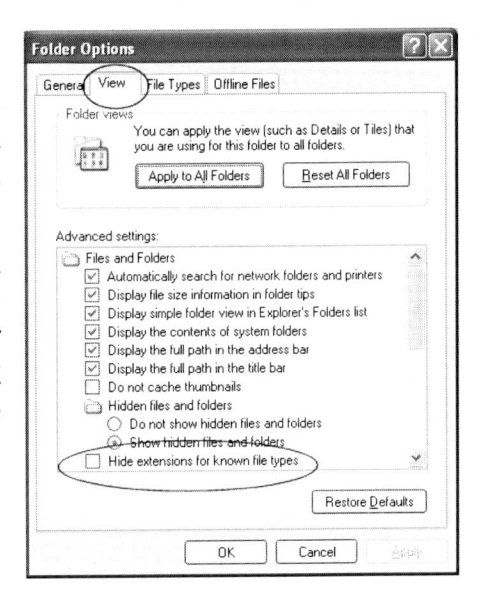

65

Changing File Associations

You may also change associations that already exist. Open "My Computer" or "Windows Explorer." Select "Tools" and click "Folder Options." Click on the "File Types" tab to view a list of file types and their associations. Locate the extension to be changed and click on the "Edit" (or "Change") option. If the program appears in the list other "Recommended Programs" or "Other Programs", select it from the pre-defined list. If it is not present, using Windows 98, click on the "Edit" button again. Choose "Browse" and select the program to be launched whenever that extension type is selected.

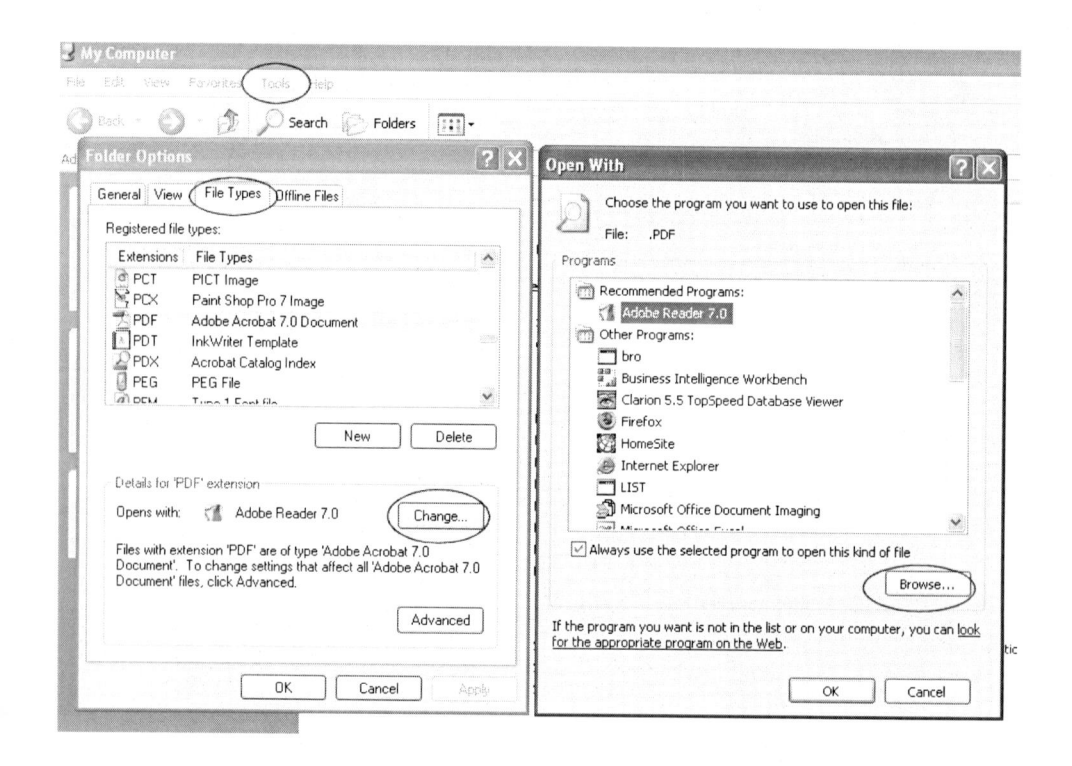

Asset Listing/Photos

An important component of future planning involves understanding exactly where you are now. In the IT world, this requires an accurate list of the equipment currently being used. This asset list should be verified and updated approximately every six months. Some IT service companies perform this "Asset Tracking" as part of their service because it provides a much clearer understanding of your operations and facilitates future service calls. A simple Microsoft Excel spreadsheet will do the job nicely if this service is not available.

The list need not be overly detailed, but should include the basic information in the event that equipment replacement is necessary. Always keep a copy of the list off-site in the event of a disaster.

Asset	Description	Serial #	Location
PC	P4, 1.7 Ghz, 256 Meg RAM, 80 BG	ATN16877	Front Desk
Printer	HP 4500 Color LaserJet	110022912	Front Desk
Router	CISCO PIX 506e	7733881A12	Server Closet

TAB Computer Systems, Inc. — Asset Listing
29-31 Bissell Street • East Hartford, CT 06108-2286

ATN	Manufacturer / Description	Additional Information
10010	Linksys / 10/100 24port Switch DSSX24	Location: RACK
10011	Linksys / 10/100 24port Switch DSSX24	Location: RACK
10000	TAB / PIII 866, 128MB RAM, 18GBHD, WIN 98SE	Location: SALES IP Address 192.168.1.30
10004	TAB / P166, 32MB RAM, 2GB HD, Win 98SE	Location: Admin
10005	TAB / P200, 64MB RAM, 2GB HD, Win 98SE	Location: S&R
10007	CLONE / Clone PII 333Mhz, 64MB RAM, 15GB HD, Win 98SE	Location: LAB
10018	TAB / PII 350Mhz, 256MB RAM, (2)8GB SCSI HD	Location: RACK

Digital Cameras

Someone once said, "A picture is worth a thousand words." Thanks to modern technology, "cheaply" could accurately be added to the end of that saying. For less than $100, you can document the contents of your business with a series of photographs admissible in court in the event of an insurance claim!

Having photos to accurately and thoroughly document your equipment is invaluable. Photos are also a wonderful tool to helpdesk support and other IT professionals when the ability to "see what you see" is necessary.

Take an hour to walk through the entire facility every year and just "snap away." Then, make a copy of the photos on a CD and store it in the software binder and drawer that were previously discussed. This is incredibly inexpensive insurance against potential questions and problems later.

TIP Use a digital camera to record current equipment configurations and always store the photos off-site.

Software Organization and Storage

Business owners don't always think of software purchases as company assets. As a result, valuable software purchases aren't always stored and cataloged in a safe manner. It is imperative that you have a logical, systematic method for tracking your software investment.

> (i) **RULE** Computer software is a valuable asset to your company. **Always** create backup images to be stored off-site. **Never** install software on systems without the proper licenses and keys.

Use this "how to" checklist to get started:

- Purchase a three-ring binder with approximately 100 CD sleeves. Store the software and license codes in the binder to be kept off-site.

- Identify a remote drawer or file cabinet for on-site storage. It does not need to be fireproof or very secure. It should, in fact, be easily accessible when necessary.

- Purchase a box of two-gallon "resealable" plastic bags to hold software. Workstation-specific software should be labeled on the outside of the bag and all media, books, etc., for each workstation grouped together in a single bag. Each file server should have a separate and appropriately labeled bag. The bags should be located in close proximity to the server. Some companies assemble a server binder containing server-specific items as well.

- At least one PC in your office should have a DVD burner and available CD burner software. Both Roxio's "Easy CD Creator" and Ahead Software's "Nero" have been used with excellent results.

- Identify one person in the company as the person in charge of managing your software copies. This person should have the knowledge and tools to create backup copies of company software. Most reputable software vendors allow the creation of at least one backup copy.

- When software is purchased online, always purchase a CD copy when available. When the CD copy arrives, immediately make an archival backup copy (ABC) and place in the off-site binder.

- Most software being distributed requires some sort of registration key or product code in order to fully install. Without these numbers, it can be difficult to easily recover from the loss of programs in the event of a hard drive crash. Always make a copy of these codes as soon as the software is purchased and place a copy in the off-site folder.

- Make a backup copy (ABC) when you purchase new software! Using burner software and blank CD's or DVD's, make a copy of each disk supplied with the software. Place the original software copy in the storage drawer and the copy in the off-site binder.

- One of the biggest software-management challenges is the seemingly constant barrage of updates and fixes that software makers require users to install on their systems. Apply operating system software updates immediately upon notification of their availability. Track and create ABCs for operating system Service Pack releases. These are usually very large files and, as such, can experience corruption on the way to your server via the Internet. If possible, go to your operating system supplier's web site (e.g., Microsoft) and see if Service Packs on CD or DVD are available. If so, paying the minimal media cost for the hard copy is recommended. It is a worthwhile investment if ever needed later. As always, create an ABC for the off-site binder.

> ⚠ **CAUTION** *Remember that even software copies are company property. Only a highly trusted employee should bring this property home for off-site backup.*

Putting IT Together

By this point, you've gotten a feel for just how important IT is to your company's daily operation and success. You know that you need to continue to invest in IT to stay on track. It's time to develop a "game plan" to be used as the blueprint for your company's IT future.

Depending on your network size (see "How Big Are You?" – page 15), you may only need a few people, and most may be outside your company. This is fine for "Small-" or "Medium-" size companies. It is essential, however, for "Large-" small businesses to focus more in-house, using employee resources with a balanced amount of external sources.

> **QUOTE** *"If we had asked the public what they wanted, they would have said faster horses."* - Henry Ford

Use the list below to confirm that you have a grasp of the IT requirements within your company.

- You have identified the players on your team and their roles
- You have an approximate dollar amount that you will spend annually on IT needs
- You have a plan for staying current (but not too current) with technology
- You've taken an organized approach to your IT assets and company data
- You have a plan for off-site documentation and software

You now have the knowledge to work with IT. In the coming chapters you will learn some specifics of the IT world and how to use even more knowledge to benefit yourself and your company.

Your Network

As a business owner, you need to play an active role in protecting your network. This may sound like an overreaction, but a safe, secure environment around the existing access to your network is paramount. For instance, if someone asks to "plug in" to access the Internet, the immediate response should be "NO." If someone asks for your wireless access password to use your network to check e-mail – the answer should be the same. These actions can impact the security of your entire company.

> **CAUTION** *Some vendors may ask to access the network for e-mail and Internet use. Unless their PC is virus and Spyware free (and you have confirmed this) – the answer must be NO! Vendors can do this elsewhere – but NOT on your network!*

Some of you may have heard stories of "war parking," i.e., people parked in the parking lot of a local company, using the company's unsecured network capabilities to download data with a notebook computer using the company's wireless Internet connection. This is happening in metropolitan areas at an alarming rate and should be a major concern to every small business owner. There are simple safeguards every small business owner should be taking to protect against potential hijacking.

Make certain to always assign a WEP (Wireless Encryption Protocol) key to your wireless network. A 64-bit key is generally appropriate. Contact the network provider with any setup questions or installation issues.

> **RULE** *Never use the default settings supplied with routers. Always "change the channel," add passwords and install WEP encryption.*

Another area of network security is password protection. Passwords should always be required for any network access. This includes passwords for sign-on, within your software applications and especially any remote access from the Internet. There is a lengthy discussion in this book under "Internet User Names and Passwords" (Page 97) that outlines various password techniques to use that applies equally to internal password design.

If you allow employees to access to your internal network outside the building (via remote access), it is imperative that you employ strong sign-on and data security access. If you cannot control **exactly** what an employee is (and is not) able to do remotely, you should not allow access at all.

Make certain that **all** password and security settings are documented into the Administrative Handbook. This information is vital in the event that you need to re-create your secure environment.

Critical Equipment Location/Placement

In order to protect your business, all assets must be protected. Correct IT equipment placement is essential for protective and longevity purposes. Refer to any liability requirements at the federal or state level as equipment location is planned (HIPAA, etc.).

Small businesses are often very tight on available floor space. Therefore, new IT equipment is often shoe-horned into existing spaces, lacking proper ventilation and protection. The following guidelines demonstrate the various acceptability levels for all IT equipment. Critical equipment, shared by multiple users and/or used to communicate with other users/network, needs specific protection. Critical equipment includes file servers, application servers, routers, switches and hubs.

The decibel, or noise level, factor should be a primary consideration when deciding where to locate equipment. For instance, equipment shouldn't be located in areas where people interact via phone, voice, etc. Higher-end equipment will invariably be louder in decibels due to increased fan/air requirements, as well as sheer size. Whenever possible, attempt to segregate important IT equipment away from populated areas and focus more on dry basements and remote closets, preferably areas that can be locked.

Use the following scenarios as a "yardstick" for your current IT environment. If lacking in particular areas, use new equipment purchases as an opportunity to improve the situation over time.

> ⭐TIP *Use a label printer to document IP addresses and machine names on equipment. Remember to include warranty expiration date and vendor from whom the equipment was originally purchased.*

Optimal Scenario

Location	Large closet or dedicated room for IT equipment – located out of the mainstream office
Windows	None
Temperature	Dedicated, year-round air conditioning unit, humidity controlled. No other outside source of heat/cooling, temperature monitored via alarm system
Power	Dedicated "home run" direct from main breaker panel – UPS on **all** equipment
Security	Locked and secured at all times
Communications	Located in same location
Environment	Clean area with little or no carpeting, low dust accumulation, low moisture, no vibration, no plumbing near area, smoke detector present and wired to alarm system
Storage	Rack mount for routers, switches, hubs, etc. Sturdy tables or racks for computer equipment. All equipment should have at least six inches of open air in most directions.
Interface	Single video, mouse, keyboard to access all equipment in the area
Wiring	All wiring neatly tied, marked and bundled. Labeled patch panels in use for all drops.

This configuration is rarely achievable in small business unless pre-planned during a move to a new site location. Remember that many of these specifications may be required due to privacy requirements, e.g., HIPAA, as well. If you are planning a move, consider all options.

Acceptable/Minimum Scenario

Location	Small or large closet space located out of the mainstream office
Windows	None nearby – preferably sealed from opening
Temperature	Air conditioning return ducts in close proximity. Heated baseboards/vents not nearby
Power	UPS on **all** equipment
Security	Locked and secured at all times
Communications	Same location or wiring clearly labeled to/from other area
Environment	Clean area, low dust accumulation, low moisture, no vibration, plumbing pipes not in proximity, smoke detector overhead
Storage	Sturdy tables or racks for all equipment. All equipment should have at least six inches of open air in most directions.
Interface	Single video with switch to access all equipment in the area. Separate mice/keyboards if needed
Wiring	Grouped together and labeled. Patch panels in use for all drops

Whenever possible, attempt to locate IT equipment in a segregated area. Secure it, via a locked closet, and protect backup media in some form of locked box or file drawer. Follow the checklist to verify that temperature, dust and vibration will not be an issue with the equipment.

Unacceptable/Potentially Dangerous Scenario

Location	In the main office area
Windows	Very close proximity
Temperature	Located on outside wall near or under a heat register
Power	No UPS in use, extension cords present
Security	None
Communications	No idea, i.e., "the phone company did it"
Environment	Vibration through floor, dust present, on carpet, plumbing pipes overhead
Storage	On the floor, located immediately next to other equipment
Interface	No monitor present – must "borrow" from another workstation to utilize
Wiring	No labeling, wires running across floor, no patch panels in use, nothing labeled or organized

It is the hope of every IT professional who arrives at a small business site **not** to see this scenario. They face the reality of not only attempting to rectify the problem, but also having to explain to the owner the dangers and risks of such setups. To be helpful, the owner can begin the conversation by stating "I know this is dangerous, and I'm committed to working with you to correct it."

Correcting this scenario will usually involve a number of contractors including electricians, phone system service personnel and IT professionals. Each one of these individuals should make an on-site inspection and provide feedback to you on the best course of correction in their particular field of expertise.

> ⭐**TIP** *If your setup looks more like the "Unacceptable" scenario above, and you are required to meet any federal or state IT guidelines, you have just failed miserably at this task. Contact a local IT firm, familiar with federal mandates, to make an on-site visit and render a compliance plan.*

The Internet - Your Business Online

As with so many topics in the IT world, there are volumes written about the Internet and its role in small business. This chapter focuses on the narrow definition of the Internet and outlines only what the small business owner might utilize on a daily basis.

> **QUOTE** *"The Internet will help achieve "friction-free capitalism" by putting buyer and seller in direct contact and providing more information to both about each other." - Bill Gates*

The Internet has replaced the "Yellow Pages" of yesteryear. Businesses without an Internet presence don't exist for many potential customers because they can't be found there. In many cases, potential customers first do a "Google" search to research companies on the Internet. Companies not found on the first page of "hits" may be deemed too small of an operation, or not savvy enough, to have a web presence. In either case, potential clients are often lost, because they will most likely give up attempting to contact you at this point.

Your Business — The Internet — The World!

Domain Names

One of the most important Internet roles is to "reach" on behalf of your business. The method for locating your business on the web, and how you are identified in e-mail correspondence, begins with your domain name. Domain names must be unique and should directly reflect the company name or product. Search engines such as Google, Yahoo and MSN will always make the name of the site appear first on search matches, so make it count. For instance, if you search for "IBM," the first entry in the found list will be www.ibm.com.

A domain name consists of a name and a Top Level Domain (TLD) suffix. Common suffixes for business web sites are *.com, .biz, .org, .cc* and *.net* (Networking Concerns). The names are also referred to as "URLs" (Uniform Resource Locators) because they convert into unique IP addresses on the World Wide Web. They are not case sensitive and may be up to 255 characters in length.

When in the process of creating a domain name, begin by compiling all appropriate possibilities. For example, if your company name is "Allied Manufacturing, Inc.," add "AlliedManufacturing.com" and "AlliedManufacturingInc.com" to the list. If your company has a specific brand name, you might also consider using it as the domain name. Interestingly, when a United States trademark is held on a particular name, the law allows you to use it as a domain name, even if another entity already owns it. This was demonstrated a few years ago, when a hamburger giant went to court and won the right to www.macdonalds.com, although it was already owned by a Midwestern plumbing company.

Once the list of possible domain names has been compiled, visit www.internic.com/whois.html or an alternate "Domain Lookup" site. These sites can determine which names are available for registration.

Your Company Web Site

Once you've identified the best available domain name for your business, it's time to make your presence known to the rest of the world. It is first necessary to *register* your domain name with a type of company called a "Domain Name Registrar" to prevent someone else from using it in the future. The quickest reference source to help you with this task is your Internet Service Provider (ISP). You can also check out companies, such as "GoDaddy" that are available to register and host your site. They include design tools integrated into their sites to get you started (see below).

Your web site will need a home, or host, located on a web server. Most often, it is hosted outside your business because of the complexities in setup, routing, etc. A web site establishes that all-important-presence on the information superhighway. Depending on your web site needs, basic content, such as hours of operation, site directions, general information about your company, and contact information may be enough to get started. Graphics or photographs are great aesthetic tools to break up the information. The following is an example of a very rudimentary site.

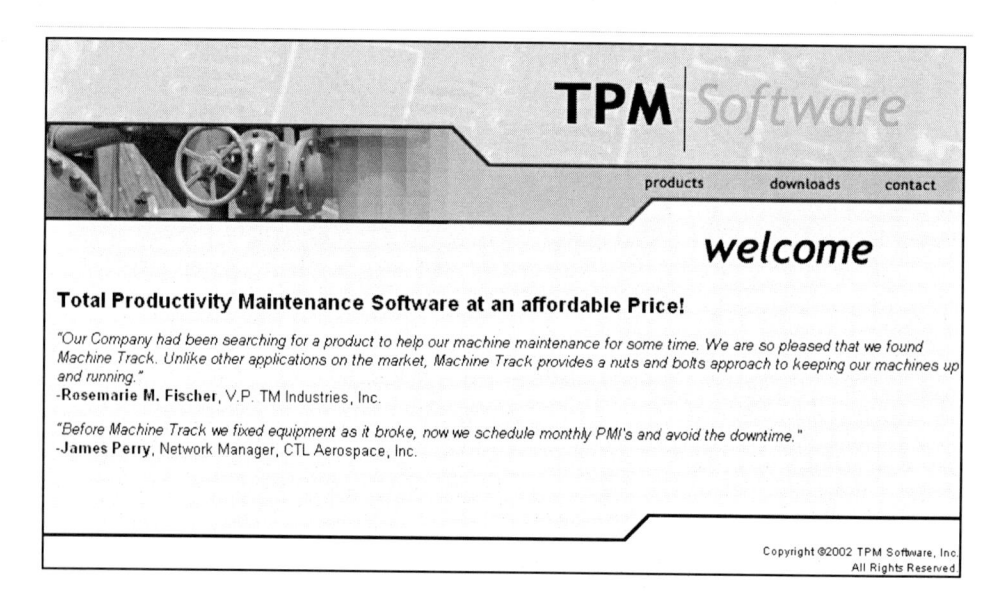

TPM *Software*

products   downloads   contact

welcome

Total Productivity Maintenance Software at an affordable Price!

"Our Company had been searching for a product to help our machine maintenance for some time. We are so pleased that we found Machine Track. Unlike other applications on the market, Machine Track provides a nuts and bolts approach to keeping our machines up and running."
-Rosemarie M. Fischer, V.P. TM Industries, Inc.

"Before Machine Track we fixed equipment as it broke, now we schedule monthly PMI's and avoid the downtime."
-James Perry, Network Manager, CTL Aerospace, Inc.

Copyright @2002 TPM Software, Inc.
All Rights Reserved.

There are some excellent resources on the web for those willing and able to build their own site. While the end result may look simple, because of the way these sites are constructed, it is an inexpensive and quick way to get started. As mentioned above, one site that caters particularly to this lower-cost alternative is http://www.godaddy.com.

Web Site "Uptime"

An important consideration when selecting a hosting company is their "uptime" percentage. Due to the 24/7 nature of the Internet, your web site needs to be available to potential customers around the clock. When companies represent their uptime, remember even if your site is up 95% of the time, this translates into it **not** being available 438 hours a year!

This represents a lot of missed business opportunity. Look for uptime percentages of at least 99%, meaning that your site is still unavailable approximately 87 hours each year. For even higher uptime percentages, there is an industry average referred to as the "five 9s rule." The maximum realistic uptime is defined as 99.999%. The 9s in the number explain the rule name. As you might imagine, the cost to achieve this standard is very high, as it involves redundant and fault-tolerant "everything." While your web presence is important, it is likely not worth the cost!

What to Look for in a Web Designer

There are a number of questions to consider in the event you are hiring a Web Designer instead. The most critical single aspect of any web site is its appearance. Therefore, it's only logical that you would start by previewing the web design company's site. Evaluate the following:

- Is the site clean looking and easy to navigate?
- Is it quick to respond to mouse clicks?
- Are some past projects linked directly to their site?
- Have they worked with other businesses, or products, similar to yours?
- Are there any testimonials on the site?
- Are "starter" web site rates provided? (Currently, $500 seems to be the small business average.)
- Will they handle both domain registration and new site hosting? Are rates provided?

For the small business owner looking for a more elaborate E-Commerce site, where products and/or services will be sold, the list of considerations lengthens. It becomes even more critical to properly prepare a precise and comprehensive strategic plan of what will be sold online. Contact Web Design companies directly by phone and discuss your project in detail.

Here's a quick list that will serve as a stepping stone for these discussions:

- Can the firm provide a pre-defined Online Shopping Cart customized for your company?
- Can you maintain your product list from a "Web-Friendly" update process or does the web design company need to be involved with all changes to your product list? You should be able to do all of this from within your "cart maintenance."
- Is there a minimum-order fee for the Shopping Cart?
- Does the firm supply Internet Merchant Accounts or is this the company's responsibility?
- Does the firm handle Certificates for the company site or is the e-commerce hosted elsewhere?

If you are considering venturing into the "Shopping Cart" world, be sure that you have a definitive list of products to be sold, including all wording, photographs, thumbnail prints (small photographs), etc. E-Commerce providers can do all of this work for you in preparation for inclusion on a web site, but the costs for the equivalent of an Online Catalog can be very expensive.

> **TIP** *Do your research prior to embarking on any online sales venture!*

While the answers to these questions may not be totally clear at this point, they will become clearer as web companies explain their options and packages. Take comprehensive notes during the initial meetings.

E-mail in Your Business

The use of e-mail in the business setting is becoming more and more prevalent. All small business owners should be using e-mail to communicate with customers and vendors. While there are some potential drawbacks to e-mail in the business setting, i.e., spam and personal use on company time, the benefits to the business are incredible.

The major benefits of using e-mail for communication purposes are:

- ✓ E-mail is more manageable. Back-and-forth communication happens more quickly, without needing to be in the same room or on the telephone.
- ✓ Utilized properly, it provides a very effective audit trail that self-documents business events and processes.
- ✓ It's simple to include multiple parties in the "conversation."
- ✓ Once sent, it usually arrives to the recipient almost instantly.
- ✓ The cost of each e-mail sent is very reasonable—virtually free.

The major disadvantages of using e-mail for communication purposes are:

- ✓ Typing lengthy e-mail replies can take longer than a telephone call.
- ✓ E-mail can be forwarded to eyes outside the company and may lead to compromised information.
- ✓ E-mail can become very impersonal and easily misinterpreted as it lacks voice inflection and personal interaction.
- ✓ Employees sometimes don't realize that grammatically incorrect e-mail reflects poorly on their intelligence and ability to communicate. They may also not appreciate that it is a direct reflection on their professionalism and company

performance. A quick review and spell check before sending an e-mail highlights virtually all errors and provides the opportunity for correction.

✓ There are potential legal liabilities from improper communication using company email as well as lawsuits that can subpoena all email archives for evidence.

How E-mail Works

Electronic Mail (e-mail) works in a very similar manner to regular mail. When an e-mail is sent, it is forwarded electronically from the

Sender → Mail Server → Internet → Domain → Recipient

PC to a mail server. The mail server reads the domain name and locates the appropriate destination address, in much the same manner as a mail-sorting operation at a traditional post office. The mail is then routed via the Internet to the proper domain. Once received, it is placed in the recipient's mail box until retrieved. This entire process can take seconds to complete.

E-mail Names

Once the decision has been made to use business e-mail, it's time to select the e-mail box name format to be used. All e-mail names are constructed as a <Name>@<Domain Name>. They are not case-sensitive and must contain the "@" between the local-part (name) maximum of 64 characters and the domain name maximum of 255 characters. When possible, the domain name to be used should be registered (see Page 81) and used for all e-mail correspondence and should reflect your business name or function.

Domain names are discussed in detail in the 'Internet' section of this book (see Page 80). The "name" part of your e-mail address should be easily identifiable, such as "tbenoit" or "sales." Avoid using any personal sounding names, such as "bigguy99" or "gonefishin2," unless the latter is used in a boat-charter service, for instance. The name should always be professional.

E-mail Subject

Always make the e-mail subject line brief and concise. The recipient should understand the contents of the e-mail simply from reading the subject line. For instance, "Meeting at 9am" although short, is not as complete as "Staff Meeting 9am Tuesday, 4/3 regarding Mandatory Overtime." Also, be careful of the "FW:" tag that gets placed in the front of forwarded e-mails. It should only contain one per subject line.

E-mail Etiquette

There are a number of web sites and book resources devoted to e-mail etiquette and the formatting and content of proper e-mails. Many contain very specific rules. Consider the basic "Top Ten E-Mail Rules" below:

Top Ten E-Mail Rules

1.) Do not identify messages as "high priority" unless they truly are!
2.) Do not write in CAPITAL LETTERS. This is the equivalent of shouting.
3.) Be concise in the subject line and body of the e-mail.
4.) Use proper grammar, punctuation and spelling.
5.) Do not attach files unless the recipient is expecting them.
6.) Re-read the e-mail before sending.
7.) **Never** reply to an e-mail when angry at the sender! Calm down first!
8.) Do not use the "Reply to All" feature unless every recipient really needs to get a copy.

9.) Do not forward anything to your entire address book, especially chain letters and jokes.

10.) Do not "unsubscribe" or reply to unsolicited e-mail in any form. That is how "spam" operators know that they have a valid e-mail address.

> ⭐**TIP** Make certain to create backup copies of contact data (address book) in the e-mail client. This is often overlooked!

E-mail Protection/Backup

If an e-mail system will be used for long-term storage, proper back up is crucial. Local Outlook Express mailbox files (with a DBX extension) are generally overlooked in back-ups and, in the case of a local hard drive crash, all correspondence is lost.

Placing the mail folder on the file server is an acceptable backup process. If Microsoft Exchange or a similar mail server is being used, the mailbox is likely, though not assuredly, on the server already. If not, move the mail folder up to the server in the "Employee" folder (see page 61, File Server Folder Structure) and modify the mail client to access it. This is a **much** safer approach in the event of a hard drive failure. When this process isn't possible, consider manually copying your e-mail folder from the desktop system onto the file server on a regular basis.

> ⭐**TIP** *The Quick Reference Guide in this book provides a step-by-step backup method for Outlook and Outlook Express.*

Synchronizing E-mail

Another method commonly used to backup e-mail data is to "synchronize" it. The methods for synchronizing data vary from e-mail client to e-mail client. Search the Internet for various ways to perform this function. In general, this technique is used when mobile users, using a laptop, receive e-mail while out of the office. Synchronizing "pushes" the e-mail back to the desktop when the employee returns to the office.

E-mail Organization

Many e-mail users treat their "Inbox" as a giant repository, storing months or even years of important documents. Imagine a desk Inbox overflowing with three years of memos and correspondence! Can you imagine three years of printed correspondence anywhere on your desk? This is exactly how many users manage their electronic Inbox. When pressed to locate a document or e-mail, the user may search via date-- *"I think I received it about three months ago,"* or by e-mail address-- *"I got that memo from Bill, yeah Bill,"* or perhaps, by subject. While newer e-mail client versions have added search capabilities, it can still be difficult to manage volumes of data. Using folders within your e-mail system is much more efficient. In the prior chapter, we discussed file server folder organization. This same technique and strategy applies to your e-mail.

Before embarking on this project, however, set aside some time to delete unnecessary mail from your Inbox. Similar to tackling the project of re-organizing the basement, it's much easier to make a sweep through the basement first, throwing unnecessary things away, before attempting to re-organize it. Export the contents of all folders first and make an ABC (Archival Backup Copy), in the event you are over-aggressive in cleaning.

Focus on the "Inbox", "Sent Items" and "Deleted Items." All popular e-mail clients allow creation of folders within the client itself. Use folders to drag e-mails from the Inbox to specific folders. Planning e-mail folder organization takes some thought on how to best organize existing records. Some common folder and subfolders groupings include:

1. "**Customers,**" with a folder for each customer
2. "**Projects,**" with a folder for each project
3. "**Employees,**" with a folder for each employee

Another popular method, also discussed with file server folders, is the "File Drawer" approach – where the existing file drawer configuration within the e-mail client is mimicked. Many variations and methods can be effective. The keys are planning and consistency.

The below example demonstrates a simple group of folders with MS Outlook Express. Experiment and try some "mix-and-match" techniques to devise the plan that works best for your company.

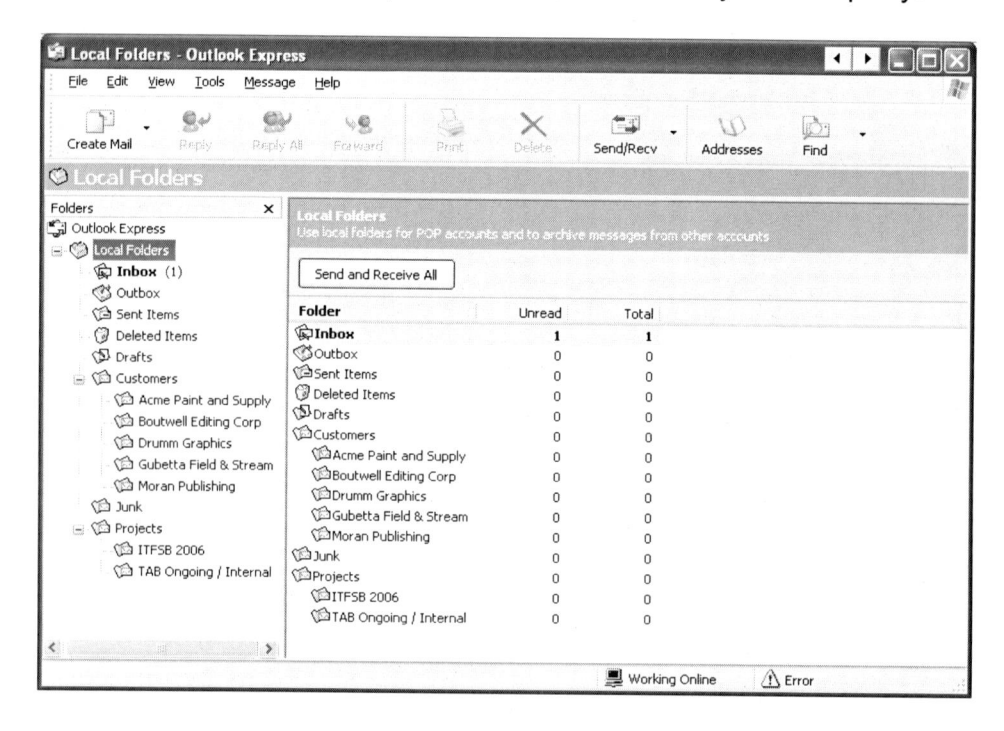

Set up "rules" within the e-mail client to automatically file incoming mail in the proper folder. This type of "rules based" input control can be extremely powerful because much of the organization is automatically done. For example, if you send customer surveys periodically and the subject line is always "How did ACME do on your printing order?", direct the rule to place all surveys in the

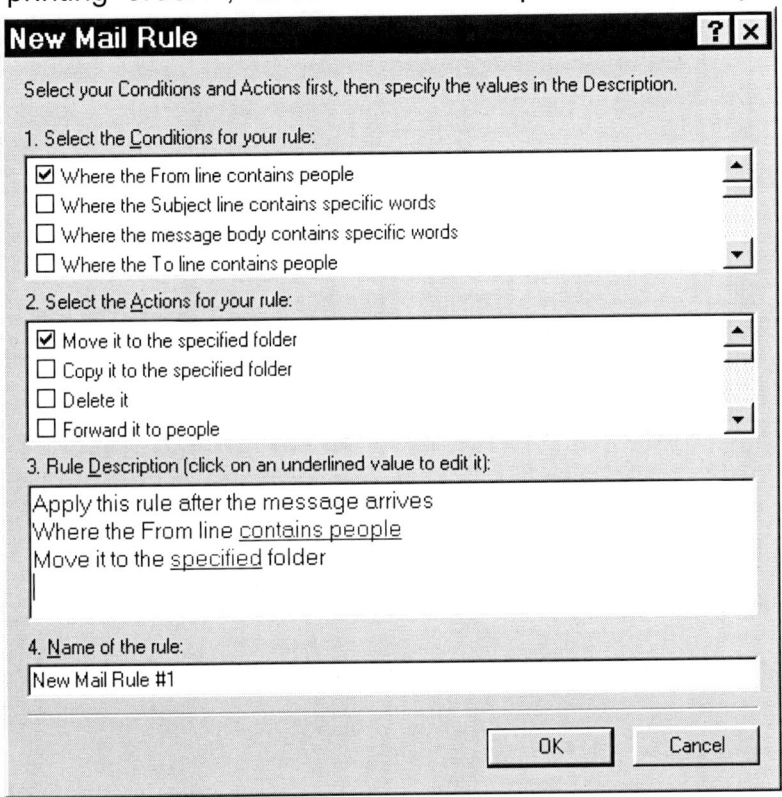

```
New Mail Rule                                                    ? X

Select your Conditions and Actions first, then specify the values in the Description.

1. Select the Conditions for your rule:
   ☑ Where the From line contains people
   ☐ Where the Subject line contains specific words
   ☐ Where the message body contains specific words
   ☐ Where the To line contains people

2. Select the Actions for your rule:
   ☑ Move it to the specified folder
   ☐ Copy it to the specified folder
   ☐ Delete it
   ☐ Forward it to people

3. Rule Description (click on an underlined value to edit it):
   Apply this rule after the message arrives
   Where the From line contains people
   Move it to the specified folder

4. Name of the rule:
   New Mail Rule #1

                                          OK          Cancel
```

"Surveys" folder. Experiment with rules with some sample e-mail. Another attractive feature is the ability to move anything that you don't want to read directly into a "Review Later" folder. This folder might include e-mail that you probably won't want to read, but don't necessarily want to delete immediately. Simply set up a rule to direct the mail on that topic straight to the "Review Later" folder. The mail can be reviewed and/or deleted later.

SPAM Filtering

Spam is defined as e-mail you receive that you have not asked for. Left unchecked, spam can fill your inbox with thousands of entries per day that need to be dealt with – even if it means simply deleting the items.

One of the biggest time savers in the business e-mail world would have to be "spam filter" software. This software can come in many forms. Online e-mail cleaning services such as "PortOne™ Clean-Mail" removes up to 99%+ of all spam before it reaches your Inbox (a few dollars per mailbox per month). Because this service is off-site, your internet connection is never "bogged down" in wasted traffic. This is currently the only service that works external to your network. Other alternatives are products that run on your PC such as "IHateSpam" from SunBelt Software (about $20 per PC). They will remove many entries from your daily review of e-mail messages. There are also hardware alternatives (appliances) such as the "Barracuda" spam filter (starting around $2000) which will remove spam, provide virus scanning and anti-spyware protection as data enters your network. All of these work quite well.

Whatever tools that you employ will save your employee's time as they attempt to do their jobs. The best advice is to use one of the tools outlined above to "stem the tide" of spam that your employees may deal with.

Web Browsers

The browser is the tool used to access the World Wide Web on the Internet. The browser has a long history and was continually modified and improved as the Internet gained popularity. There are predominantly four Internet browsers used today, and all do an excellent job. There are, however, subtle differences between them that may make their functionality better or worse for some small businesses.

Internet Explorer (IE)	The most popular, therefore the most targeted by hackers
Mozilla Firefox	Not as prone to viruses, spyware and viruses
Opera Browser	The fastest browser for quick page loads
Apple Safari	Perhaps the safest of all, but has a number of compatibility issues with many sites

For occasional Internet access, any one of the browsers listed above will be fine. However, the Internet Explorer browser is more prone to spyware, pop-up window displays and hijacks (explained below).

Spyware started out innocently as a way for marketing companies to track which web sites were being visited. As you would visit a site, a "cookie" (a small package of data) was written to your hard drive indicating that you had been to that site. It recorded what pages you looked at, how long you stayed on each page, etc. Then as you re-visited the site, it would send that information back to a marketing firm for analysis. It was very innocuous in the beginning and users really didn't notice the intrusion. A good program that will show you these types of "cookies" is Ad-aware by Lavasoft. You can find a free version of this software at http://www.lavasoftusa.com. When you install and run it, you'll be amazed at how many of these it will find (and optionally remove).

Other forms of spyware are placed on your system as a "Trojan horse" (i.e. they pretend to be one type of software when they are actually another). Examples of this are web sites that offer to clean up spyware when in fact, they are spyware themselves! This is the most common method of spyware installation.

> (i) RULE *Never allow a Web site to install software on your system unless you have specifically asked to have it installed.*

Pop-Up windows are sub-windows that appear when you visit certain web sites. All recent versions of browsers have done an admirable job of eradicating these annoying screens. The control of this feature is usually located under the "Tools/Options" menu of the browser.

A browser hijack mainly occurs in Internet Explorer. The other top 3 browsers do not support a feature called a "Browser Helper Object" (BHO) which is how a hijacking program takes control of your browser. Microsoft added the BHO feature to allow programs to interact more directly with their browser. However, it quickly became abused by hackers and used maliciously. An example of a "good" BHO is the Adobe Acrobat reader plug-in for Internet Explorer. It allows you to read Acrobat PDF files just by clicking on them in a web page. An example of a "bad" BHO is one that starts every time you access the Internet and takes you to sites that you don't want to visit. The latter is the most common form of hijack technique and also the toughest one to remove.

The advanced troubleshooting section of this book will step you through the removal of these types of issues.

Many "surfers", those who spend hours each week surfing the Internet, use Mozilla Firefox as their main browser. The advantages of Firefox are many:

- ✓ It is not as prone to security breaches (because some of the functionality doesn't exist).
- ✓ It seems to be a faster browser.
- ✓ Password management is more robust.
- ✓ The "tabbing" feature is exceptional (which is due out with IE 7 version).
- ✓ Pop-up management is well executed.

> ★TIP *Use Firefox or Opera when surfing. It's generally safer and faster!*

You can download a free copy of Firefox at http://www.mozilla.com or a free copy of Opera at http://www.OperaSoftware.com

Some web sites have been customized for Internet Explorer browsing only, forcing the surfer to switch over to IE for site access. This is usually noticeable when you expect a page to be filled with graphics or have additional functions and they appear to have "empty space." If a web site does not "look right", try to view it using Internet Explorer. It may then appear correctly.

> **Mid-State Motors, Inc.**
>
> *Mid-State has been around for almost as long as automobiles have been in existence. Over the years they have embraced automation at all levels because their supplier required it. While not entirely sure of the rewards, they spent the money because that's what "corporate" required them to do.*
>
> *When "corporate" released their newest version of software that was Internet-based, Mid-State decided to equip every PC and terminal in their Network with access to this version and replace their "dumb terminal" access. Mid-State management also thought that it be a good idea to allow access to the Internet and E-mail as part of this upgrade. While it certainly seemed like an instant "winner" for productivity, it quickly backfired into an X-Rated, shopping-spree-infested, instant-messaging, spam-choked world.*
>
> *The company found itself investing in online virus protection and spyware solutions, as well as a way to regulate sites visited by employees on a moment-to-moment basis.*
>
> *This foray into the online world cost the company more than twenty thousand dollars in special software, hardware and personnel related costs. Their access to their parts and repair database, while now Internet-based, did not improve or change since the upgrade.*

As you can see, while it is generally good to keep up with technology, there are also pitfalls to doing so. The PC has replaced the telephone in terms of "time wasted" at work. Without properly monitoring activity, this account was headed for some huge losses in productivity and efficiency. The cumulative effects could have been devastating. Remember that if forced to upgrade, all of the potential pitfalls should be addressed first.

Internet User Names and Passwords

Every computer user has been there. You're trying to access your credit card Web site to get your balance. You're at the "Log-in Information" screen and have absolutely **no** idea what either your log-in or password are, so you give up and call them! There are a few simple methods to avoid this inconvenience.

Unsecured Method 1: Have your browser store all user names and passwords in its internal system. Firefox does a great job with this because of its Internal Password Manager. Microsoft Internet Explorer does a fair job because it uses a "cookie" storage method. Either browser can expose password information quite easily. Only information originally stored on the computer is accessible. This won't help if you are accessing sites from other computers or locations.

Unsecured Method 2: Create a password protected file on the desktop, containing a list of all accounts, user names and passwords in a single file. Information is then easily retrieved while online and portable enough to be e-mailed to other locations, such as home. The pitfall, again, is that the file is not secure and can easily be copied by others. Hackers have little difficulty breaking password-protected files.

Combination Method: Many sites require a sign-on or log-in simply to get a valid e-mail address for marketing and solicitation purposes. For **all** such sites, where you don't care about the information behind the password, always use your business e-mail address and a simple 8 digit password of your choosing. Some sites require a "hardened" password, one that contains combinations of letters, numbers and special characters. Most sites have a minimum and maximum length requirement. A minimum of 8 alphanumeric characters (letters and numbers mixed together) provide the safest passwords. Create something simple like your first initial and your date of birth, with a special character at the end of the string. For example, "Tj051260@" or "bF031688@" will usually satisfy any site requirements. You now have a hardened password to use in conjunction with your standard business address to use for almost all sites you might visit.

For those sites where you care about the information that lies inside once you have entered your password (such as Banking and Credit Card sites), creating a secure password becomes a bit more complicated. Continue to use your business e-mail address for all log-in/user names. For those sites requiring account numbers for access, you will need to revert to "Unsecured Method 2" for the account number. Never include the password in that file, just the account number along with a vague label along with it. For example, if you access your AllState Policy online, use "Life Insurance N00031666." Never include AllState in the password.

For **all** passwords, use this format: Initials@MMYYxXxX

Initials	The initials of your first and last name
@	The "@" symbol
MMYY	Your birth month and year
XxXx	The first four letters of the site in upper and lower case

Examples: tb@0560BaNk   Bank of America Password
            tb@0560AlLs   AllState Insurance Signon.

This strategy should be modified to your particular style (change the special character, position, order, etc.), but the intent is to create a password environment that is unique and easily remembered. Incorporating part of the site into the password, i.e., "AlLs," makes it both unique and simple to remember. Never share a specific password approach with anyone.

Shared Passwords – Not Secured

There are times and situations when sharing passwords with co-workers may be appropriate. If this is a common practice, the above methods should not be used. Instead, select a common object or animal and suffix it with the current year. It's always a good idea to "harden" it by capitalizing the first letter. The reality is, since you are sharing it with others, it really isn't that secure. For example, use "Fox2006" or "Tuna2005." Pick a few objects to use so, if the password is forgotten, there are only a few combinations to try.

Password Changes

Some sites require periodic password changes. Others even "pattern test" the password string to keep it unique from others you have previously used. Unfortunately, there is no way to circumvent this, and you may need to resort to Method 1 for storing these passwords. For those not so strict, use the Combination method and add a number to the end of your current password bringing it to nine digits.

Backup Your Data

If the hard drive malfunctions, and most will after some period of time, only a valid backup will get you up and running again. Imagine the lost productivity and frustration if **all** data in the current computer system needed to be re-created. Backing up the file server in a systematic and reliable method is as critical a business decision as paying the electric bill. Without doing both, the likely consequence is being out of business for some period of time.

> (i) **RULE** It's **your** data. If not properly backed up, you're responsible for the consequences. Assign reliable staff members with the actual process to ensure that it is done correctly and accurately.

Backing Up Data Correctly

Utilize an internal SCSI DAT tape drive for backups whenever possible. This type of tape drive is highly reliable when compared to other more inexpensive drives. Ideally, it should be large enough that multiple tapes are not required for backup. You should own at least six tapes, with two spare tapes, as well as a tape cleaning cartridge, labeled as follows:

MONDAY, TUESDAY, WEDNESDAY, THURSDAY, FRIDAY-1, FRIDAY-2, CLEANING

The rotation itself is quite simple. Insert the appropriate tape in the drive by the end of each work day. Alternate the FRIDAY tapes from week to week. This ensures a "snapshot" of at least two weeks in the event that a file is inadvertently deleted. The

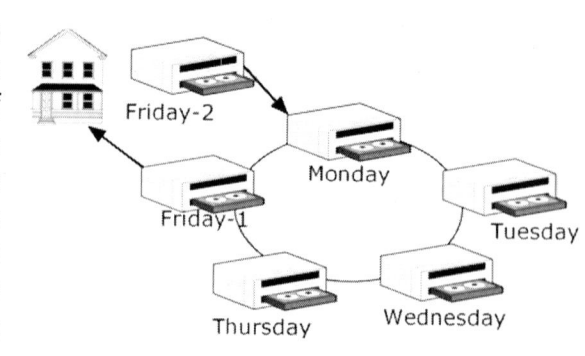

"FRIDAY" tapes should be stored off-site and returned to the office on the day needed.

Tape software should be configured to run unattended at night (Monday through Friday). Running tape backup at night ensures that users will not be holding any open files on the server. Remind all users to exit all programs on their workstation when leaving for the day. This is critical, as many backup systems do not back up open files.

Assign someone in the office to verify that the nightly backup has been successfully performed, and be certain there is a backup person trained for the responsibility in the event that the person assigned isn't available. Remember to validate that the backup is working properly. If tapes are being switched without validating, chances are excellent that there isn't a valid backup.

> **(i) RULE** It is not enough to just swap tapes on a nightly basis. **Read the backup logs** and be certain the backup was successful before changing the tape each night.

Address any log errors found. For instance, some system files are always locked and cannot be backed up without shutting down certain system services. Examples of this would be Microsoft Exchange work files and databases or, in the example below, IIS log files. At times, users do not exit all of their Windows and leave a

```
Backup of "W: \\DC-TAB\c$"
Backup set #4 on media #1
Backup description: "daily Sun-05-01-2005-7-30p"
Backup Type: Copy

Backup started on 5/1/2005 at 8:38 PM.
Warning: The file \WEB\LOGS\MSFTPSVC1\ex0604.log in use - skipped.
Warning: The file \WEB\LOGS\W3SVC1\ex0605.log in use - skipped.
```

file open on the server. These errors can usually be corrected by speaking to the appropriate user to have them exit from all of their open applications before leaving for the day. As a general practice, it would be advisable to e-mail the log file to your computer support company so they can verify if these files are required and if a potential problem exists. If in doubt, call support rather than ignoring potential problems.

> (i) **RULE** Always assign a password to your backup tape set. It is acceptable to use the same password for all tapes, though it should be very unique from other passwords.

If many month-end functions are performed, consider a three-tape rotation, with a backup at the end of each month. Label the tapes as follows:

MONTHLY-1, MONTHLY-2, MONTHLY-3

Only the most recent monthly tape should remain on-site. If data is isolated to specific folders and doesn't exceed 650 megabytes, you could also utilize a standard CD-BURNER to gather the "snap shot." This is the process used at TAB at the conclusion of each month-end cycle. You also have the option with current technology to burn (make a copy of) a DVD with up to 4.3 gigabytes of data per DVD. This can also be upgraded to 8+ gigabytes utilizing "dual layer" technology, meaning that even most large database applications can use a "snapshot" approach to backups as well.

The following is an example of what can happen when a backup plan is implemented, but not verified:

Case Study: Pegasus International
Pegasus employed an in-house IT specialist. However, after some difficult business downturns, the decision was made to eliminate the internal position and outsource it.
The outsource firm found a server solution utilizing mail order servers with a RAID-5 storage system. They were shown extensive documentation with a 25-tape rotation and off-site backup scheme. It appeared the former IT specialist had left them in good shape. However, the outsourced firm

> never validated the backups or performed a test restore to verify that they were working properly. After all, they had a meticulously maintained 25-tape rotation in place.
>
> Soon, the main file server reported a disk drive error. The server was under warranty with the mail order company. Their technician was sent to replace the drive. When he arrived, he needed to replace other hardware (backplane, etc.) as well. They were replaced and he left Pegasus with a server and a "bare bones" operating system (no data). The technician never confirmed that there was a valid backup.
>
> The outsourced company arrived to restore the data. They reinstalled the tape software and inserted the first carefully labeled tape from the set. After running a catalog, the tape appeared to be empty. They checked the checked tapes #2, #3, and #4 from prior days – all empty. They continued and finally found data on tape number #24-- a single backup image of data more than six months old. It was worthless...
>
> There were no drives to send to a data recovery firm, as the mail order technician had retained them. There was no local data backup. The client was left with an empty shell of a server and the prospect of total manual re-entry of their data. And that is exactly what was done...
>
> It's your data. It's your business. It's your responsibility to make certain it's properly backed up.

Use a cleaning cartridge approximately every two to three months. The process only takes a few minutes and extends the life of the tape drive, as well as the life of the tapes. In addition, the cleaning increases the likelihood of good backups. Many DAT tape drives have a yellow "clean" light that illuminates when the drive requires cleaning. Never ignore the yellow light. Immediately place the cleaning cartridge in the drive and allow it to perform its function.

Most tape manufacturers recommend replacing tape sets every six to nine months. However, annual replacement is fine if a tape cleaning cartridge is used. Naturally, in the case of a bad tape and an unsuccessful backup, the tape should be replaced immediately. Be certain to have spare blank tapes on hand at all times for these occasions.

> ⓘ **RULE** **Never perform incremental backups.**

Some users will utilize an incremental backup. This method of backup only captures data on the hard drives that has changed since the previous backup operation. This increases the possibility of introducing faulty media on a restore because you need to restore the last full backup set first and then apply each incremental tape in reverse order. This practice is not recommended!

It is also not a recommended practice to backup workstation data onto a server-based backup. Treat the server backup as its own entity. To centralize backup, create server folders for each user to be used for document/central storage. As a general rule, users should never store company data on local computer hard drives.

There are some exceptions to this rule. For example, some payroll services require information to reside on a local PC. In this instance, a separate tape backup system should be installed for each local PC. It should be running a scheduled unattended backup job each night. While more expensive to do this, it provides the safest option available. A very conscientious user could also utilize a DVD burner as the backup media.

> ⓘ **RULE** **When using DVD or CD for backups, do not use rewritable media. Burn a new copy with each backup.**

Continuous Data Protection Servers (CDP)

A new combination of device and service is just appearing in the IT market. A CDP Server is a device that continually makes a backup copy of your file server and workstation data. This data is available for instant restore if needed. The Server also "versions" the files, keeping multiple copies available on the disk as needed. This is helpful in the event that an older copy needs to be retrieved. Unlike tapes, it is stored on hard drives.

Another highlight of this technology is its implication for off-site backup. The data can be streamed via the Internet on a "real time" basis and your important data can be archived off-site. This will

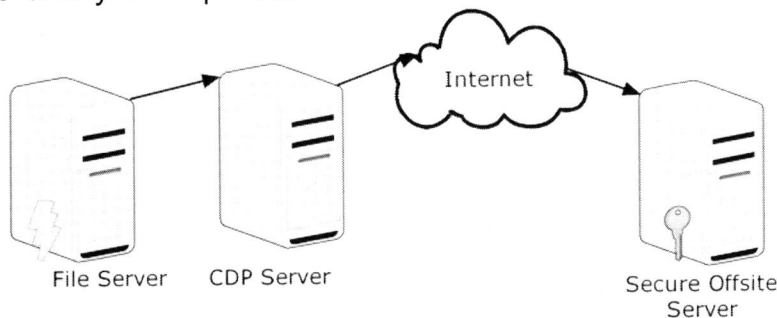

File Server — CDP Server — Internet — Secure Offsite Server

become increasingly popular for Disaster Recovery Implementation.

There are also "bare metal" restore options in the event of a total server failure. A completely empty file server can be restored to a prior working state with a single, push of a button, action. Most other methods of restoring a file server typically require a multiple step process and many hours before the server is back online.

This type of technology can drastically change the standard methods of safely backing up valuable company data. Ask local IT providers about this emerging technology.

Workstation Imaging

Another emerging technique for protecting workstations is imaging. This technique involves a "client" that runs continuously on local workstations and a "NAS" (Network Attached Storage) device. As data is modified at the local workstation, changes are written, or pushed, to the NAS device, keeping a complete image intact on the device. In the event of a virus or system crash, this image can be written back once repairs have been made.

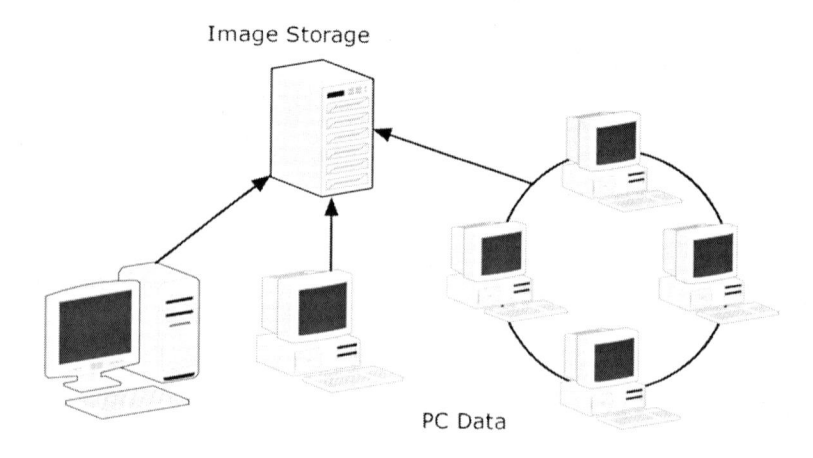

This technique can be useful if data is stored locally, or with custom desktops and user profiles on workstations that would be difficult to recreate. However, remember that valuable data should be stored on your file server and not on workstation hard drives whenever possible.

Case Study: Able Accounting Group, CPA firm

It was 9 a.m. on April 14, 2001. The Able Accounting Group was working at a frenetic pace to complete client returns by midnight on April 15th. The tax paperwork was churning out of the two 15-page-per-minute laser printers, being collated, bound and placed on the accountants' desks for final review and mailing. Suddenly, all equipment stopped working. All PCs froze, both printers went off line and stopped. No one had a clue as to why.

One of the partners entered their server room to find a disk failure "Novell" error. He immediately realized the firm was in a serious predicament. He placed a call to his local computer support company and explained what he was seeing. The support company realized the gravity of the situation and promised to respond within the hour. They did.

The support technician arrived with a spare hard drive from inventory and replaced the faulty disk drive. Since the faulty drive was used for the accounting system and not for the

Novell operating system, he was able to initialize it and get it back online very quickly.

The technician asked the client for the latest copy of backup tapes, which had been meticulously maintained. However, unlike the tapes from the Pegasus Corporation mentioned in another case study, these were checked and verified on a daily basis. The technician initiated the restore at 10:30 a.m. on April 14th. By 11:45 a.m., the tax data and system were restored to the prior night. The firm re-entered the tax data that had been entered prior to the 9 a.m. crash, and by 12:15 p.m. the firm was completely operational.

Lessons Learned:

1. Always be certain that you have a valid backup by whatever means possible.
2. When evaluating IT support firms, focus on finding one that has been instrumental in making things happen. Don't shop for a computer company that can come in and fix minor problems. Shop for one that can come in and "save the day" when it really counts.

Disaster Recovery Planning

Rarely does a small business owner have response plans for any type of disaster recovery. Imagine a very large tornado, an F5 class, suddenly appears. Now, imagine that tornado hitting your building with 300 mile per hour winds. It flattens your building and destroys 100% of your IT equipment, as well as everything else in your office. A normal response might be, "Well, if that happens, data recovery is the least of my worries!" Not quite. If there isn't off-site data, it is now 100% gone - forever. It's not retrievable in any way. Data is not like the office desks, chairs or computers, which can all be replaced by writing a check. Data generally can't.

Use the following simple checklist to begin crafting a Disaster Recovery Plan. Most items are covered in more detail elsewhere in this book so, if the other internal systems have been implemented, the basic IT worries are already covered.

√	Disaster Recovery Detail
	Verify that the existing tape drive used for backups is still available for purchase. In many instances, tape drives become obsolete and, if unavailable for purchase, backups might be unreadable! Also be certain to have a current backup copy of tape software off-site. Without it, it is not possible to restore data from tape!
	Assign someone in the office to take the "Friday" tapes from the server home every Monday and return them on Friday (in a rotation).
	Once monthly, burn a new DVD of the most critical data folders. Take it home and leave it there. It is **very** cheap insurance.
	Keep an archival backup copy (ABC) of all software off-site.
	Make print screens and print outs of network equipment configuration off-site and on-site. If you are unsure how to do this, ask your IT service company to do it for you.

	Take an inventory of computer equipment once every six months to maintain an accurate inventory. Most IT service companies will perform this task. This inventory list will be critical in the event of needing to replace equipment quickly. Keep a copy of this list off-site.
	Be sure that you have a local hardware vendor available to expedite purchases. They should be able to get you back in business quickly with a detailed inventory list. Sometimes there may be temporary equipment, i.e., notebook computers involved.

There are a number of excellent books on Disaster Recovery and Business Continuation Planning available. One insightful resource is *disaster RECOVERY planning* by Jon William Toigo. Small business owners should contemplate necessary actions to get back up and running in all business phases, including manufacturing, operations and accounting. The IT implications are only one piece of the puzzle. As remote as it might seem, the possibility for fire, flood or other catastrophic events could seriously cripple any business.

> **TIP** *Remember, it's all about protecting your business.*

Off-site Reciprocity Agreements

Many large companies, even ones in direct competition with one another, arrange reciprocal agreements in the event of disaster. If, for instance, Company A loses its IT capabilities for some reason, they can go to Company B to restore their data and attempt to get back online. Consider a reciprocal agreement with any other company with a little extra space. Of course, the agreement would be mutual. Usually for small businesses, the agreement is simply an "office space" arrangement, and doesn't involve actual equipment for backup/recovery, though agreements can be customized on many levels.

Disaster Prevention Planning

The old adage "an ounce of prevention is worth a pound of cure" is especially true in the IT world. Just a few simple tips and tricks can prevent catastrophic things from happening. Again, most of the tips below are covered in more detail within the various sections of this book.

Disaster Prevention Checklist

√	Disaster Prevention
	Have an "Electrical Fire rated" ("BC" type) fire extinguisher in very close proximity to critical IT equipment, as well as one located approaching the location.
	Place a thermometer close to critical IT equipment. If the ambient temperature is above 80 degrees for an extended period of time, equipment is in danger.
	Check the server fans and test air flow monthly.
	Check switches and hubs for overheating issues monthly.
	Never place critical IT equipment near a window. If this position is unavoidable, place under a table.
	Follow a daily/weekly/monthly checklist for normal maintenance items.
	Watch for lights that dim for no apparent reason near equipment. They can indicate power fluctuations, which is very unhealthy for equipment. See the "power" section of this book for more specifics.
	Check all outlets used for critical equipment for loose plugs and/or new equipment that might be causing an overload. Items such as space heaters should never be near critical IT equipment.
	Make certain that the tape drive has "verify" turned on. This is imperative when test restores are not performed on a regular basis.

Terminated Employees

A large potential risk to any business is the departure of an employee. An employee can leave with much more than a handshake and well wishes. In order to protect the business, create a concise checklist to use with terminated employees. The checklist should include:

For the Employee:

> **Data Release and Disclosure** – This document contains very strong legal wording that the employee must sign at termination. It states that the employee has no company data in his/her personal possession, and that all data is the sole property of the company. A sample follows.

> ### Sample Data Release Form

> | |
> |---|
> | This is to certify that I do not have in my possession, nor have I failed to return, any documents, data, customer lists, customer records, sales records, or copies of them, or other documents or materials, equipment or other property belonging to the Company, its successors and assigns.

I further agree that, in compliance with the Employee Proprietary Information Agreement, I will preserve as confidential all trade secrets, confidential information, knowledge, data or other information relating to products, processes, know-how, designs, formulas, test data, customer lists or other subject matter pertaining to any business of the Company or any of its clients, customers, consultants, licensees or affiliates.

Dated_____

Signature
THIS IS NOT A LEGAL DOCUMENT |

For the Business:

- ✓ Disable the user's account on the file server.
- ✓ Remove the user's name and/or password from every software package that utilizes them.
- ✓ Disable the user's account from any remote access via the Internet.
- ✓ If a VPN was utilized, change the password if shared.
- ✓ Reroute the employee e-mail to supervisor.

> ⭐ **TIP** Keep in mind that many MP3 and portable music players (iPods, etc.) can be used like a disk drive, and unscrupulous employees could save sensitive company data on them. They could easily move data off-site without your knowledge.

Disposal of Data

Most offices and small business owners are now acutely aware of the need to shred printed documents of all kinds. Identity theft is a growing concern all over the world and shredding all documents, rather than throwing them in the trash, is a must.

Properly disposing of paper correspondence is only part of the larger data disposal issue, however. Due to technology advances, important data can be located on a number of media forms, all of which must be properly disposed when no longer needed.

The only safe data destruction method is to render the media unusable. Software formatting and "fdisk" removal are all potentially recoverable operations. It is critical that the media **never** be used or read again.

How to Destroy Sensitive Data

CD's/DVD's	There are shredders available that will do a great job of rendering CD's and DVD's unreadable. They may also be broken in half manually when wearing eye protection.
USB Flash Drives	These solid-state devices should be smashed with a hammer when disposal is necessary. Always wear eye protection.
Diskettes	These can be broken in half or open the diskette metal door and slice the media with scissors multiple times.
MP3 Players	Most MP3 players have a "disk" mode which would allow anyone to directly copy files from your systems. Where possible, these should be destroyed in a similar fashion as USB flash drives.
External USB Hard Drives/Internal Hard Drives	The safest way to render these unreadable is to simply open them and expose the disk platters to the air. Leave them exposed for approximately 30 minutes and the disk surface will be unreadable. To be certain, bending a platter or pulling on the read/write heads will forever make the drive unreadable. A little dirt tossed in for good measure also works quite well.

When disposing of PCs, take the time to disassemble them and render the media unusable. The time spent is a great investment when compared with the potential consequences of not taking these precautions.

When disposing of other peripheral items, i.e., printers, verify that all media cards have been removed from the media slots, if so equipped. Some users use media cards as an alternative storage device, as well as images, etc. This sensitive information must also be located and rendered unreadable.

Other IT devices, i.e., routers and switches, do not contain sensitive information, although they may contain configuration information and passwords that have been used. If you are disposing of them, take a hammer to these also. Monitors, keyboards, and mice may be safely disposed with no precautions.

Charitable Donations/Computer Recycling

There is **no** way, short of destruction, to know for certain that all valuable information has been removed from a disk or any other media. Some companies donate their equipment to worthy causes and, understandably, receiving a PC with a smashed hard drive is of no value.

For companies interested in making charitable donations, there are a few software shredder programs available, such as "CyberScrub." There are also "Shred & Delete" options available in Symantec and other vendor's products. Utilizing a shredder program, re-formatting the hard drive, and reinstalling the operating system is a relatively safe process to expunge all data.

File Server – Why Do I Need One?

The primary reason for utilizing a server configuration is consolidation of data and security into a single entity. Since company data is so critical and sensitive, it should be held in a *repository* that is backed up on a regular basis, preferably nightly. It should also be mirrored with software or hardware, to make certain more than a single copy exists at any point in time and to provide protection with security layers.

A peer (P2P) environment, using one PC as a central repository, can be used if working with small amounts of data or word processing files. This type of environment is also suitable for very small offices with less than five extremely conscientious users and a rock solid data backup plan.

According to Iron Mountain, a data backup and recovery firm, **more than 60% of critical company information** is located on laptops and PCs, rather than the appropriate file servers. Focusing on a server-based approach to data storage is the safest way to protect your data!

File Server versus Workstation – What's the Difference?

Some business owners tend to think of a user's PC, or workstation, and a file server as the same thing. While both are computers, the similarity ends there. If a single PC fails, usually only one employee is directly affected. If the file server fails, usually **everyone** in the company is affected and the down time is much more costly. For that reason, file servers should be more heavy duty. The following is a quick comparison of the two, including their average configuration:

	Workstation	File Server
Case	Any size is fine	Mid-Tower minimum
Cooling	Power, CPU	Case Fans(2), Power, CPU
Memory	256 megabyte	1 gigabyte
Disk Drives	SATA (1) 7200rpm	Mirror SCSI (2) or RAID-5 (3),10,000 rpm
Operating System	Windows XP Professional	Windows 2003 Server
Backup System	None	Tape with automatic scheduling

By definition, file servers must have at least two disk drives that mirror each other. There is also a feature that utilizes three or more RAID-5 drives to provide additional redundancy. In either case, if a disk drive fails, the file server is able to continue operation. The disk drives need much higher rotational speeds to transfer data from and to several users simultaneously. This is also the reason for increased memory in the server.

Figure: File server with five fans, redundant power supplies, RAID-5 drives, Dual CPU configuration

As a rule, PC's built as file servers also contain higher grade components, such as the Motherboard, ECC RAM, SCSI Drives and controllers, etc. A file server will cost more initially, but consider the extra cost an investment. While the temptation may be to save money on the purchase, always select a quality computer with top shelf components from a reputable company.

> **Down Time Calculator**:
> Single PC (non-critical): Lost Hours * Overhead Cost per Employee * 1
> Example: (4 hours * $25.00) * 1 = **$100 lost production**
> File server: Lost Hours * Overhead Cost per Employee * # of Users
> Example: (4 hours * $25.00) * 10 = **$1,000 lost production**

The potential exposure with server issues is much higher than with a single PC and, as such, should be factored into your purchasing decision.

> ★ TIP A $1,000 computer is **not** a $2,000 computer at half price!

File Server Software

While there are several operating systems available for small business file server use, Windows 2003 and Windows 2003 SBS are the most common. In order to comply with Microsoft regulations, it is important to purchase the correct number of seat licenses. All service packs and updates should be applied before the server goes "live" on the network.

It is also critical that virus protection be incorporated on the file server. It should be installed prior to being attached to the network.

There are other alternative operating systems available such as Unix or Linux that can be utilized. However, you need to weigh your business survival in the mix here. If you do not have direct support for these operating systems on an ongoing basis (college students typically love to set these up for small business – and then go back to school), it means that you have just exposed your business to

ZERO support in the event of a problem. Weigh this decision carefully. *Remember, it's not about cost, it's about success...*

> ⭐TIP Never "surf" the Internet on your file server. Only access the Internet for software updates from known vendor sites while on a server browser.

Remote Server Monitoring

As technology evolves and becomes more readily available to small business owners, complexities also increase. Some companies, we here at TAB for example, offer remote, affordable monthly file server monitoring. The server(s) check in with the remote service periodically and report important statistics:
- Event Log Irregularities
- Virus Issues
- UPS Status
- Disk Space Usage
- Backup Issues
- Operating Statistics

For more information about TAB Computer Systems' Remote Server Monitoring options, visit http://www.patroldog.com

Maintaining Your Network – Do it Like the Pros!

The "trick" to keeping everything running smoothly in a small business network is as simple as having a daily checklist:

Network Management Checklist

	Description	Who?
Daily	Check server backup logs	
	Rotate tapes – insert new tape	
	Check for messages/warnings on server monitor	
	Check external lights on UPS for battery issues/loads	
Mondays	Return prior week "Friday" tape, removing current one off-site	
	Check virus scanning software – run full scan	
	Check for Windows Updates if automatic updates are not enabled	
	Check available disk space on all volumes, cleaning up if less than 500 megabytes	
	Perform a test restore of a sample file from a prior day's backup	
Monthly	Shut down and restart server	
	Create archival backup via monthly tape or DVD – removing to off-site	

> ⚠ **CAUTION** *Remember that all off-site materials are proprietary to the business. Only a very trusted employee should be given this critical assignment.*

Power – How Important is It?

Obviously, all PC's, even notebook computers, require power to operate. Even more importantly, "mission critical" PC's, and every file server, require "clean" power, or power that has been intercepted by an "**U**ninterruptible **P**ower **S**upply" (UPS) and conditioned to optimal voltage levels. Consider automobile fuel. While the lowest octane fuel might be appropriate for a personal vehicle, a high-performance car demands higher octane fuel for ideal operation. It may operate for a short period of time on lower octane, but eventually the motor will take enough abuse and parts will begin to fail. The same analogy is true for power!

> (i) RULE **Always** keep mission critical PCs and all file servers plugged into a working, fully charged UPS. **Never** plug laser printers into a UPS!

Sudden power interruption to a critical PC or server can cause data corruption and operating system failures. In more serious instances, disk drives can completely fail or crash, rendering the system unusable. All these situations are easily avoidable.

While the UPS will keep the computer up and running for a brief period of time, it also needs to be intelligent enough to tell the server when shutdown is necessary. Use software that runs on a file server to "listen" for UPS power warnings. If the UPS detects lost power, it will inform the server and the server will begin an orderly shut down of the operating system.

Another major advantage of this software is for battery monitoring. The software measures battery levels and will notify the server if a battery needs replacement. While battery technology continues to improve, most UPS batteries have a useful life of approximately 24 months.

Most UPS models have indicator lights that display battery strength, as well as the current UPS power load. It's good practice to check these periodically.

> ★TIP **Many** file servers are installed with a UPS, but without properly running monitoring software. Verify that the monitoring software is running and schedule a weekly UPS Self Test.

As a rule, it is always best practice to use a UPS between every PC and wall outlet. If this is not practical, there should be a surge protection power strip used for protection from major power surges.

> ⚠ CAUTION Never plug a PC directly into a wall receptacle. Always protect mission critical equipment.

If your business experiences frequent short-term outages of one to three hours, there are certain UPS configurations with additional batteries that will facilitate keeping the systems operational. This will, however, lead to the need for extended "up time" for workstations, network switches, firewalls, and the telephone system. This can get quite costly in terms of replacing batteries, given their relatively short lifespan.

An alternative to consider would be a generator with enough wattage to safely power the IT equipment. When utilizing UPS equipment for all mission critical equipment, an "instant on" generator isn't necessary. Rather, a stand-alone unit with a power transfer panel will provide enough time in a power outage for the battery power to shut down equipment gracefully. You can then start the generator and cut over to that power source. When utility power is restored, simply reset the panel to the utility source and stop the generator.

Contact a certified electrician to discuss business needs for generators and their effectiveness. They will be familiar with the necessary wiring requirements, load calculations, and generator placement planning.

Workstation Specifications

It can be very confusing to quantify the best type of workstation to purchase for many reasons. The type of software to be utilized, the required software speed, and other factors should all play a role in the decision.

What is **not** difficult to quantify in any business environment, is reliability. Computers used for business must be as reliable as possible. Computers should have a multi-year on-site warranty from a reputable company and should be constructed of name brand components. Also, business PCs should not be running any home software, i.e., Windows XP Home, Norton personal edition, etc.

Remember, this is a business PC to be used for important business functions. Look no further than the "Dependence" chapter of this book (see Page 16) to be reminded of the true PC value. It's not the cost of the equipment, it's the cost of a failed PC to be considered when purchasing. Be willing to pay a little extra for the peace of mind of knowing it can be up and running quickly – not days or weeks later.

Notebook Versus Desktop – Which One to Buy?

This is an ongoing discussion between computer professionals and users. There are pros and cons for both sides regarding effectiveness, cost justification, etc. In general, the best advice is to weigh the advantages and disadvantages of both before making a decision.

Notebook Disadvantages:

- Expensive compared to desktop systems – usually twice the cost
- Easy to misplace/steal
- Higher breakdown rate
- Not easily repairable

- Keyboard not ergonomically friendly
- Easier for company data to be compromised/copied
- Tendency for users to install "non-company" applications
- They cannot perform within the same price/performance as desktops. You are paying for portability, not performance.
- Upgrade path is very limited regarding hard drives, additional RAM, etc.
- They have a tendency for obsolescence with peripherals (auto adapters, spare batteries, etc.)

Advantages:

- Portable, with remote connections to office, etc.
- Useful for entertainment (DVD, music, GPS, etc.)
- Power savings as they consume less power than desktops
- "Mobile Office" with pertinent data at users' fingertips

A notebook is probably more viable if a mobile office is a necessity. Weigh the need carefully. In many cases, the notebook won't be making many, or perhaps, any trips out of the office and money has been spent unwisely.

In all cases, it is recommended that you shop for a notebook via a SuperStore such as CompUSA or Best Buy. They should have a number of display models to "test drive" prior to a purchase. The feel of the keyboard, the control of the touch pad, etc., all play a role in proper notebook selection.

When a notebook is purchased, be certain to purchase any and all accessories at the time of purchase. For instance, buy the spare battery, auto adapter, airplane adapter, etc., immediately. It is best to always have two batteries on hand. Also, look to maximize the hard drive size and the installed RAM. Consider purchasing the extended warranty, if available. Be certain to research warranties carefully.

Another consideration option for notebooks is the refurbished or recycled market. Many corporations sell their "retired" units via a local store or Internet. Very low-cost notebooks are frequently available at affordable rates. A buyer who does proper research can often get the best of both worlds – a powerful desktop for office use, and the portability only found with a notebook.

The Wrap Up

At this point you will be feeling a bit overwhelmed at the amount of information that has been tossed your way. Most small business owners would not take the time to absorb this topic at a level that has been presented. You deserve immense credit for getting to this point!

The book has been laid out in such a way that you should be able to use it as a reference tool. Use the Glossary or the Index toward the end of the book to look up unfamiliar IT terms and acronyms. Use the Table of Contents to identify major topics, such as file servers or power considerations. Reread certain chapters as needed. Eventually, this will all make more sense as you increase your exposure to and familiarity with IT.

What was covered in this book? What are the points that you need to take away from reading this? The recap below should help to focus on the material covered and what you can "glean" from this. Take a moment to see if the points made in the book stuck with you:

- Identify the possible pitfalls in your IT strategy and avoid them!
- Identify "who does what" in your IT world
    - Build your list of responsibilities
    - Be sure that your employees understand your IT policies
- Calculate how much money per year IT is really costing your company
    - Come up with a rudimentary budget for the coming year
    - Create an Asset listing so that you can plan PC replacement/upgrades in a consistent manner
    - Review the criteria for acceptable equipment location and placement, strive to improve the operating environment around it
- Workstation guide
    - Notebook / Desktop comparisons
- File Servers – compare them correctly

- Organize the folders on your file server for ease of use
- Use simple file names for easy identification
- Power management

+ Implement new technology and software upgrades with care
    - Use a checklist to confirm the safety of a software upgrade

+ Determine your employees skill set level as it influences IT
    - Develop an IT training plan once you know your needs

+ Review your current internal third party software use.
    - Consider a "vertical market" package

+ Build an "administrator's" handbook that clearly documents your IT environment

+ Get your company presence on the Internet
    - Get your "name" on the Internet
    - Build/Buy a company web site

+ Use e-mail to your advantage
    - Always follow the Top 10 e-mail rules
    - Organize your incoming e-mail
    - Get SPAM protection

+ Control your company's use of the Internet
    - Practice "safe surfing"
    - Protect your company from spyware, pop-Ups, hijacks
    - Use passwords - the right way

+ Disaster prevention and disaster recovery
    - Backup strategies that work
    - Use a digital camera to document your IT environment
    - Create off-site copies of your software programs and documentation
    - Terminated employees - protect yourself
    - Final Disposal of IT equipment / data

Quick Reference

The following section details the "Quick Reference" guides included in subsequent pages. These are useful when making changes to the IT environment or when experiencing specific problems that may have a quick fix.

Reference	Purpose
Basic Installation Considerations	Useful for additions and upgrades to your network
Quick PC Troubleshooting	Quick tutorial to identify PC problems
In-Depth PC Troubleshooting	The real nuts and bolts
Internet Issues Troubleshooting	Problems with connecting to the Internet
Browser Troubleshooting	Browser hijacks, spyware, etc.
E-mail Troubleshooting	Quick tutorial of settings, etc.
Printer Drivers	Installing on Windows 2000/XP
Backing Up Outlook/Outlook Express	Instructions for making a backup copy of e-mail data

Basic Installation Considerations

It's always helpful to any technician/installer for the client to be prepared for an upcoming installation. The following checklist will assist in proper planning for many types of IT installations.

- ✓ **Down Time** – While a technician is working on a major server or key workstation installation, the company may experience time when the network is not available. Plan accordingly and inform employees that the network will be affected during the upgrade. Plan, as best as possible, for the necessary time allotted to perform the upgrade as down time.

- ✓ **Scope** – Small business owners should be certain to review the project scope to be performed. It is not unusual for items that didn't seem pressing during the planning phase to become critical months later during the actual installation. A comprehensive review of expectations needs to occur in order to make the best decisions regarding hardware and software purchases.

- ✓ **Critical Application Software** – Have all media, documentation, and proper technical support numbers available prior to installation day. Contact application providers and inform them of the upcoming installation. They may offer tips or configuration requirements that need to be performed in a specific order for proper upgrade. They may also offer insight as to just how long the upgrade will take. It is your responsibility to gather any software keys, passwords or registration information required to complete an installation.

- ✓ **Basic Server or Workstation Parameters** – Most companies use a standard server and workstation configuration. The technician will need to know if the server name, administrator user name, password, volume partitions, and terminal server mode are unique. This information needs to be received prior to their equipment preparation. Discuss any questions and unclear issues with the application software support persons as soon as possible. Be clear and specific about what data may need to be transferred from one machine to another. It takes approximately one hour per gigabyte to move data from system to system. Plan accordingly.

- ✓ **Environment Considerations** – Always verify that there are at least two electrical outlets available within 10 feet of the installation site for each piece of equipment being installed. Verify that there are holes or conduits in place to route keyboard, speaker, monitor and mouse connections. Keyboard and mouse placement will require a clear workspace approximately 24-26 inches wide and 12 inches deep from the edge of the keyboard. Verify that there is a network connection available within 15 feet of each file server, workstation or printer. If adding additional network equipment, verify that there are enough available ports.

- ✓ **Review of Server Upon Completion** – Work with the on-site technician to understand:

    - Where the data is located
    - How the Smart-UPS works. Ask for a demonstration.
    - How the server backup works and how to verify it has worked by checking log files
    - How the server virus files are updated and how to verify
    - How your disk manager operates and how to check it for integrity

Quick PC Troubleshooting Guide

Below is a very generic PC troubleshooting list. By following the steps below, a majority of PC problems can be quickly and accurately diagnosed. Before starting, verify that all valuable data is backed up multiple times, on multiple media. Do not go any further until multiple backups exist.

1. Use Google to research specific error messages, i.e., "Failure in C55SRVX.DLL" or "Error 27372."

2. Verify that virus software is completely up to date. Install any engine and/or DAT updates. Run a full scan of all hard drives.

3. Verify that there is sufficient disk space (at least 500+ megs) available on the primary partition (usually C:). If not, run disk cleanup. Consider uninstalling unused programs to reclaim more space.

4. Check hardware for malfunctioning or slow-spinning fans. The inside of the PC should not be hotter than a comfortable summer day. If it feels like Death Valley, there is probably a temperature issue. Make certain all dust is removed from the PC intake areas.

5. Disable all power saving features, both within Windows and also in the BIOS system. Reboot once everything has been turned off.

6. Disable any screen saver software. Remember that, in order for a screen saver to work, it needs to monitor every keystroke and mouse movement to know when to "wake up." This can cause unwanted problems.

7. Check the Windows Update site and be certain that every patch and update is applied. This includes Media Player, IE,

etc. Only "Language" support module patches/updates don't need to be applied.

8. Delete any temporary Internet files from the browser. Never delete files manually from the hard drive. Set all security settings back to "default" or "low" within the browser.

9. Download and run Adaware by LavaSoft. You can find the free home version of the software at http://www.lavasoftusa.com. Make certain to check for updates as soon as the software has been installed. It is located on the first screen above the "Next" button. Just like Viruses, new spyware comes out frequently and requires updates.

10. Run a ScanDisk and Defragment your hard drive. The simplest method to run both utilities is to boot computer in "safe mode" and run it. Then, re-boot when you complete to return to normal mode.

11. Disable any software firewall, such as Zone Alarm or Black Ice, the moment it causes any issues. At this point in the debug session, look for anything that could interfere with the proper operation of a PC.

12. Ask whether any new hardware of software has been recently installed. Have any problems occurred since installation? If so, uninstall or use a "restore point" to restore system prior to original installation. Professional help may be necessary to perform this operation.

In-Depth PC Troubleshooting Guide

The following is a more in-depth look at troubleshooting. These steps should be performed only when **very** comfortable with making operating system setting modifications.

1. Check the "Device Manager" for any yellow exclamation points that appear in the tree. If present, start by removing

    the devices in error and re-booting the system. Driver CDs may be required. There may be a red "X" over a device as well, indicating that it is disabled or has failed. Enable the device for possible correction.

2. Run MSCONFIG. Click on the "Startup" tab and uncheck every listed item. Reboot the machine. If the problem does

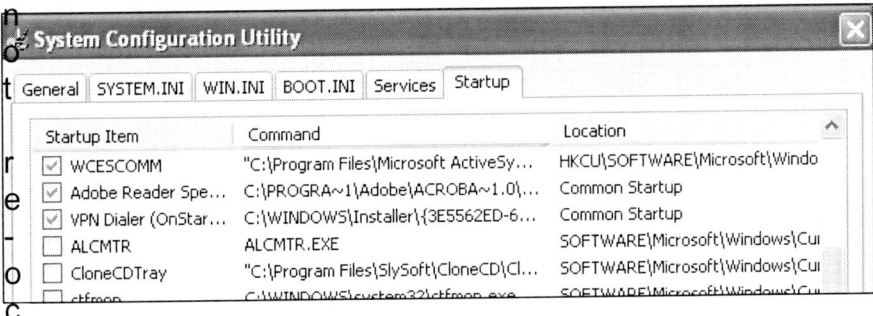

    not re-occur on reboot, it has been isolated to a startup problem. Follow the instructions to recheck all items again and reboot. It is normal for some devices to now be missing from the list. Return to MSCONFIG and recheck the items

133

one at a time, re-booting in between to identify the process causing the problem.

3. Device Drivers – At times, certain device drivers can get corrupted and cause sporadic problems. It may be time to start updating video and printer drivers. This can be done safely from the "Device Manager."

4. In an attempt to get the system functioning again, review the available system restore points and pick one to fall back to. Bear in mind that you would probably need to install some missing software, etc., that may have been installed after the restore point selected.

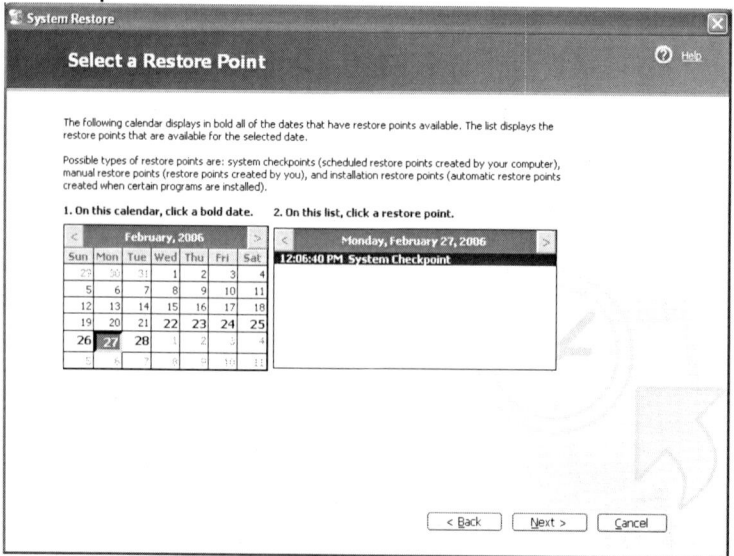

5. Running a system repair at this point would be the last attempt to avoid a complete "wipe and reload" of the operating system.

6. Registry Cleaning should be reserved for this level of diagnostic and/or fixes. "Registry Mechanic" seems to be a good tool, but must be purchased in order to get full functionality.

7. If all other attempts have been exhausted, it may be time to consider a complete "wipe and reload" of the operating system. Remember, this is an **absolute last resort**, and should only be performed after you have copied as much data as possible from the existing drive / configuration onto backup media.

Internet Troubleshooting Guide

Follow these steps when experiencing Internet connectivity issues:

- ✓ Verify that "link" lights are displayed and blinking on the network interface card. View the connection where the network cable attaches to the PC. Verify that the cable is secured on both ends. If the PC network cable plugs into the wall, check that end as well. If there are labels on the wall data connection, make certain there is a "link" light at the other end of the connection.

- ✓ Verify that the cable or DSL modem is blinking and showing signs of activity. If not, the connection may be down.

- ✓ Check the network cable between the cable/DSL modem and the router to confirm that it is seated firmly and clicked securely in place.

- ✓ If there is also a switch or hub involved, verify that the cable between the router and the hub is also connected firmly and clicked into place. Verify that the hub also has green lights and power.

- ✓ Go to a command prompt and attempt to "ping" a known IP address. If a response is received such as *"Reply from 68.142.226.32: bytes=32,time=..."*, your connection to the Internet is working. Rule out hardware failure as a potential suspect.

```
C:\WINDOWS\system32>ping 209.101.83.1

Pinging 209.101.83.1 with 32 bytes of data:
Request timed out.
Reply from 66.6.64.130: Destination net unreachable.
Reply from 66.6.64.130: Destination net unreachable.
Reply from 66.6.64.130: Destination net unreachable.

Ping statistics for 209.101.83.1:
    Packets: Sent = 4, Received = 3, Lost = 1 (25% loss),
Approximate round trip times in milli-seconds:
    Minimum = 0ms, Maximum = 0ms, Average = 0ms

C:\WINDOWS\system32>ping 68.142.226.32

Pinging 68.142.226.32 with 32 bytes of data:
Reply from 68.142.226.32: bytes=32 time=32ms TTL=49
Reply from 68.142.226.32: bytes=32 time=31ms TTL=49
Reply from 68.142.226.32: bytes=32 time=31ms TTL=49
Reply from 68.142.226.32: bytes=32 time=32ms TTL=49

Ping statistics for 68.142.226.32:
    Packets: Sent = 4, Received = 4, Lost = 0 (0% loss),
Approximate round trip times in milli-seconds:
    Minimum = 31ms, Maximum = 32ms, Average = 31ms

C:\WINDOWS\system32>
```

✓ Again, at a command prompt, try to "ping" an address using a name. Use www.yahoo.com. (PING www.yahoo.com). Lack of response could indicate a DNS error and ISP or internal IT support staff should be notified.

```
C:\WINDOWS\system32>ping www.yahoo.com

Pinging www.yahoo.akadns.net [68.142.226.32] with 32 bytes of data:
Reply from 68.142.226.32: bytes=32 time=32ms TTL=49
Reply from 68.142.226.32: bytes=32 time=31ms TTL=49
Reply from 68.142.226.32: bytes=32 time=32ms TTL=49
Reply from 68.142.226.32: bytes=32 time=32ms TTL=49

Ping statistics for 68.142.226.32:
    Packets: Sent = 4, Received = 4, Lost = 0 (0% loss),
Approximate round trip times in milli-seconds:
    Minimum = 31ms, Maximum = 32ms, Average = 31ms

C:\WINDOWS\system32>
```

Browser Troubleshooting Guide

When experiencing browser issues, try these steps as possible corrective actions:

- ✓ For persistent browser problems, download and run *SpyBot Search and Destroy*. Please be aware, however, that *Spybot* can remove more than intended.

- ✓ *HiJack This* is the next weapon in the fight against Browser Helper Objects (BHO). This utility should only be used by those knowledgeable with all computer aspects. For those less than totally comfortable, follow the instructions to post *HiJack This* results to their forum and let other, more experienced, users provide feedback and suggestions.

- ✓ Microsoft also has a method for disallowing any BHO to run. Remember that good BHO's, i.e., Google Tool Bar, will not be permitted to run either. For that reason, it's not a recommended option.

Troubleshooting Tips for Other Scenarios

E-mail Just Stopped Working

There are many reasons why e-mail stops flowing in and out of the office. Outlined below, are various scenarios that may occur:

Multiple office computers that cannot receive or send e-mail

- ✓ Verify that there is still Internet connectivity by attempting to browse a site.
- ✓ If running a mail server, verify that it is up and running properly.
- ✓ Connection to the Internet or the Domain Name Services (DNS) of the ISP can be eliminated as the issue if using "POP" mailboxes and able to surf. There is a strong possibility that the ISP mail servers are down for maintenance or experiencing a problem of some sort. Retry the operation every 15 minutes on various workstations. If the problem persists, call the ISP and request a status report.

Multiple office computers and only one cannot send and/or receive e-mail

- ✓ Verify that there is still Internet connectivity by attempting to browse a web site from the affected workstation.
- ✓ Verify that the user name and password are correct.
- ✓ Verify that the POP and SMTP server names are correct.
- ✓ TAB allows users to use a test account on our mail server. Set up an account to access the following configuration: Servers: **SMTP:** mail.tabinc.com **POP** : mail.tabinc.com **User name:** test **Password:** test
- ✓ Attempt to send and receive an e-mail to/from this account. If successful, the problem lies with the ISP and, most likely,

the account itself. Contact the ISP to inquire about the status of their mail servers and your account in particular.

Local Printer Won't Print

If a printer connected directly to a PC won't print, check the following items before calling for help:

- ✓ Verify that the printer is plugged in and powered on.
- ✓ Make certain that the printer cable on both the computer side and printer side is plugged in firmly.
- ✓ Verify that the paper path is clear of debris and any small pieces of paper. Look carefully inside and all around the paper path.
- ✓ Make certain that a printer is defined and that a default printer is selected. Look at the printer icon for black checkmarks to verify both.
- ✓ Select the default printer by double clicking. When the queue appears, locate any pending print jobs. Review the top line of the queue window. Does the printer description line have a "paused" or "offline" text message?
- ✓ In the Printers folder, select the printer. Right click and select "Properties." Click on the "Print Test Page" button. Does a test page appear?

Installing a Windows Printer Driver

Almost all new printers include CD installer programs. Use installer programs when available. If not, use the guide below to assist in installing a new printer.

USB Printers (Windows 98 and newer)

1. Locate the printer on the web by using "Google" to locate the printer model and the words "software driver."

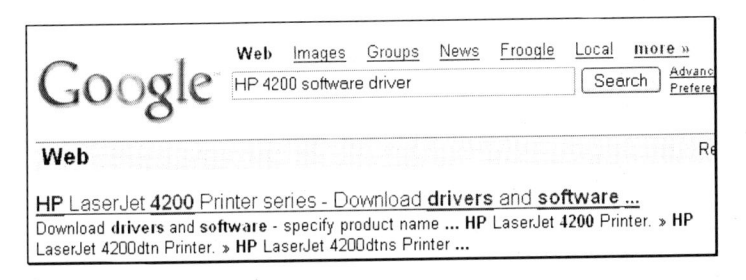

   ![Google search for "HP 4200 software driver" showing result: HP LaserJet 4200 Printer series - Download drivers and software]

2. Once the correct drivers have been downloaded, plug in the USB cable and power up the printer. The "Add New Hardware Wizard" windows installation program should appear.

3. Click "Next," then "Search for the best driver for your device." Click "Next."

4. Clear, or uncheck, the checkmarks beside all options except "Specify a Location." Click "Browse." Browse to the disk, CD, or directory where your printer drivers are located. Click "OK," click "Next" twice. Click "Finish."

5. Turn on your printer. Windows should show a small USB icon in the system tray and the printer should be online. Print a test page. Click "Finish."

Parallel Port Printers (Windows XP)

1. In Windows XP, from the Start menu, select "Printers and Faxes", then click "Add a Printer" under Printer Tasks. Click "Next."
2. Select "Local printer attached to this computer." Click "Next."
3. Click "Use the Following Port," letting XP determine the LPT port to use.
4. Select the manufacturer and model for the printer to be installed. If it does not appear on the list, attempt to choose a "closest match" which may work. If not, search the web for a suitable driver. Use "Google" and type in the printer model and the words "software driver" to search.

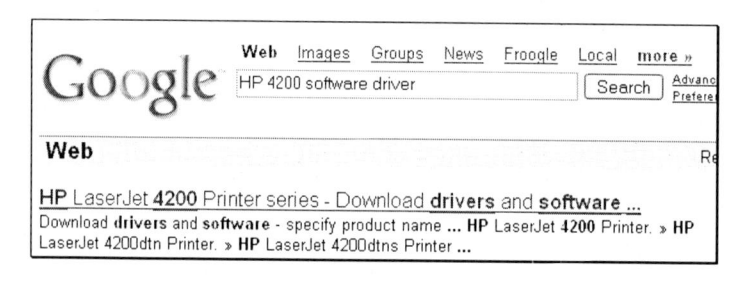

```
Google   Web  Images  Groups  News  Froogle  Local  more »
         HP 4200 software driver              Search   Advanc
                                                       Prefere

Web                                                         Re

HP LaserJet 4200 Printer series - Download drivers and software ...
Download drivers and software - specify product name ... HP LaserJet 4200 Printer. » HP
LaserJet 4200dtn Printer. » HP LaserJet 4200dtns Printer ...
```

5. Change the name of the printer to be meaningful. Select "Yes" to make certain it is the default printer.
6. Select "Do not share this printer." Click "Next."
7. Print a test page to be sure that your printer is working properly. Click "Finish."

Making a Backup Copy of Your E-mail Data

Backing Up Microsoft Outlook Express Data

- Load Outlook Express.
- Select Tools/Options/Maintenance from the Outlook Express Menu.
- Click the "StoreFolder" button.
- Note the name of the directory that contains mail files (or highlight the name and use Ctrl-C to copy).
- Exit out of Outlook Express.
- Navigate using Windows Explorer (right click "Start," select "Explore") to the directory noted above.
- There will be files with a **.DBX** extension located in that directory.
- Copy (**don't move**) those files onto your file server, a separate hard drive or external CD/DVD.
- You now have a valid archive of your e-mail messages.

Backing Up Microsoft Outlook Data (without Exchange)

- Open Microsoft Outlook.
- Right click on "Personal Folders."
- Select "Properties."
- Click the "Advanced" button.
- Note the name of the directory that contains your **.PST** file (or highlight the name and use Ctrl-C to copy).
- Exit Outlook.
- Navigate using Windows Explorer (right click "Start," select "Explore") to the directory noted above.

- Copy (**don't move**) those files onto your file server, a separate hard drive or external CD/DVD.
- You now have a valid archive of your E-mail messages.

Backing Up Additional Outlook Information

Outlook also has other file types stored in the same directory as the **.PST** file. Use the reference list below to back up any other data important to save.

Type of Data	Extension
Personal Folders	.pst
Outlook Bar Shortcuts	.fav
Rules Wizard Rules	.rwz
Nicknames	.nick
Signatures	.rtf, .htm, .txt
Stationary	.htm
Templates	.oft
Dictionary	.dic

Glossary

ABC	Archival Backup Copy – an image of software or data that is created and immediately removed off-site for safekeeping.
Bandwidth	The capacity of a communications channel such as an Internet connection. The higher the number, the more information the channel can carry at once.
"bare metal" restore	The restoration of a file server and all its data from backup media including all hardware settings/configuration.
Broadband	A way of transmitting large amounts of data including video and digital traffic over a single communication media (typically DSL or Cable systems)
Burn	Slang for making (burning) a CD copy of information such as music, software, or data backups.
Calc	A calculator program included with all current versions of the Windows OS
Case Sensitive	A term that refers to letters of the alphabet used in a way that upper case and lower case letters have different meaning i.e. CaSe is not the same as case
Client	In software terms, the recipient of data from another source
Comptia	**Comp**uting **T**echnology **I**ndustry **A**ssociation – responsible for computer exam administration and compliance.
Configuration	An arrangement of hardware and software designed to accomplish a task.
Control Panel	An area of the Windows operating system that allows the user to configure and customize their environment
Cookie	A small text file of information that certain Web sites write to a user's hard drive while

	the user is browsing the Web site.
CPUA	**C**ost **P**er **U**ser **A**nnually - A method for calculating and establishing the cost of IT
DAT	**D**igital **A**udio **T**ape - A tape format that allows large amounts of data to be stored on a single tape
Decibel	A method of measuring a sound level - the higher the number, the louder the sound
Device Driver	A form of interface between hardware and software
Down Time	The time that IT resources are unavailable to employees to perform their job
DSL	**D**igital **S**ubscriber Line – A method of high-speed communications that utilizes existing copper telephone wires. DSL lines can carry both voice and data simultaneously.
DVD	**D**igital **V**ideo **D**isk - Plastic media containing 4.3 gigabytes of data in a single layer, 8+ gigabytes in a dual layer
FireWire	Apple Computer's version of a high performance serial bus, (similar to USB) that connects devices to your personal computer.
Firmware	Specialized software usually pre-programmed on chips to bridge the gap between hardware devices
Freeware	Software offered "as is" for you to freely use and distribute at no cost
FTP	**F**ile **T**ransfer **P**rotocol - a program used for sending and receiving data from computer to computer
Gateway	A device (usually a router or Firewall) that acts as a funnel to move data in and out of the Local Area Network
Google	An Internet-based search engine site
Hardware	What remains when the electricity has been unplugged from a computer system

HIPAA	**H**ealth **I**nsurance **P**ortability and **A**ccountability **A**ct - enacted by Congress in 1996 requiring electronic transfer of information and more controlled privacy of patient records
Hot Fix	A software correction (usually related to operating systems) that addresses a small area of code
IM	Instant Messaging – an easy way to converse with a friend or colleague who is currently connected to the Internet.
Infrastructure	The physical equipment (computers, servers, wiring, etc.) that make up a computer network
Interface	A connection between two computer devices, either hardware or software based
ISP	**I**nternet **S**ervice **P**rovider - A company or entity that provides access to the Internet
Mirror	Redundant Hard Drive Configuration – also known as RAID-1
Mission Critical	A term used to define areas in business that simply cannot fail or can only fail for a brief period of time
Network	Combination of hardware and software that interconnects your system with other hardware and software
Notepad	A simple text editing program included with all current versions of the Windows OS
Novell	A software company that pioneered Local Area Networking with their Netware OS
Off-site	A location not on or near the primary residence of the company
Operating System	Software used to control and operate a computer
Peer (P2P)	Peer to Peer - A networking design that shares equipment and data, generally without a central server

Peripheral	An external device that attaches to a computer
PPPoE	**P**oint to **P**oint **P**rotocol **O**ver **E**thernet - Used by DSL as a communication protocol requiring User Names and Password for access
Print Screen	A method of printing out the displayed screen image to a printer. This is usually accomplished by a combination of keystrokes from the keyboard.
Rack	A storage system usually 19 inches in width that allows IT equipment to be stored compactly
RAID	**R**edundant **A**rray of **I**ndependent **D**isks. Redundant Hard Drive Configuration – RAID-5
Repository	A facility where items can be deposited for storage or safekeeping
ROI	**R**eturn **O**n **I**nvestment - The actual value received over time for an expenditure
Router	A network device used to route data in and out of a network
SATA	**S**erial **A**dvanced **T**echnology **A**ttachment - Hard Drive Interface
SCSI	**S**mall **C**omputer **S**ystem **I**nterface - Hard Drive or Tape Drive Interface
Server	In software terms, the sender and supplier of data to other sources
Service Pack	A collection of software corrections. Usually Service Packs are cumulative in nature, in that every new service pack contains all corrections from prior Service Packs as well
Shareware	Software offered using the "try before you buy" concept
Shortcut	An icon used to quickly access an individual procedure or program
Software	Commands that instruct the computer to

	perform certain tasks
Software Upgrade	An update to an application that modifies or enhances the functionality of the software
SOP	Standard Operating Procedure. Usually a group of documents outlining the Standards by which an organization operates.
SPAM	Junk Mail sent to you without your permission
Spyware	Software placed on your computer without your permission that tracks your movements on the Internet and can potentially take over your computer
Switch	A network device that controls the flow of information within a Local Area Network between devices
TCO	**T**otal **C**ost of **O**wnership - A method for calculating the Total cost of an IT investment over its entire lifetime
Telecommuting	The process of working from your home while connected to the computer network in your office
Thumbnail	A smaller version of a graphic on a web page (usually a photograph) that allows the viewer to link to a larger version
UPS	**U**ninterruptible **P**ower **S**upply Battery Backup/Power protection
USB	**U**niversal **S**erial **B**us - a connection method/protocol/Interface for attaching devices safely and easily to a computer
Vertical Market Software	Software designed and built for a specific industry
WEP	**W**ireless **E**ncryption **P**rotocol - Used by wireless networks to make the data sent wirelessly more secure
WordPad	A simple Microsoft word processing program included with all Windows

World Wide Web | Operating Systems
The portion of the Internet containing sites of data, linked together by references to each other

Bibliography

TechTarget -
http://whatis.techtarget.com/definition/0,289893,sid9_gci214023,%2000.html

"A 5-Step Guide to Protecting Backup Data." IronMountain.com.
<http://www.ironmountain.com/US/knowledge/protection/5 stepsprotectdata.pdf>.

Anderson, Kristin and Carol Kerr. <u>Customer Relationship Management</u>. New York: McGraw-Hill, 2002.

"Application Software." Wikipedia.
<http://en.wikipedia.org/wiki/Application_software>.

Bailey, John Taylor. "Why is Total Cost of Ownership (TCO) Important?" Darwinmag.com.
<http://www.darwinmag.com/read/110103/question74.html>.

Bruce, Anne and James S. Pepitone. <u>Motivating Employees</u>. New York: McGraw-Hill, 1999.

"Build the Most PC for Your Money." Extreme Tech.
<http://www.extremetech.com/article2/0,1697,1644128,00.asp>.

Burns, Kathy. "Organizing Your Email." InsideOffice.com.
<http://www.insideoffice.com/insideoffice-20-20021007Organizing-Your-Email-.html>.

"Computer Components."
<http://www.comptechdoc.org/hardware/pc/begin/hwcomputer.html>.

"Desktops vs. Notebooks." PCGuide.com
<http://www.pcguide.com/buy/req/detNotebooks-c.html>.

Devaraj, Sarv and Rajiv Kohli. <u>The IT Payoff</u>. Upper Saddle River, NJ: Prentice Hall, 2002.

"Email Etiquette." Emailreplies.com.
<http://www.emailreplies.com/>.

Emigh, Jacqueline. "Total Cost of Ownership." computerworld.com.
<http://www.infotechnet.org/ntca/Costs.htm>.

"Environmental Factors." Electronic Specialists, Inc.
<http://www.elect-spec.com/faqenviron.htm>.

"Filenames and Associations in Windows." PCWorld Malta.
<http://www.pcworldmalta.com/archive/iss58/filenames.htm>.

"Fire Extinguisher Types." Fire Extinguisher: 101.
<http://www.fire-extinguisher101.com/>.

"Harness E-Mail: How It Works." Learn The Net.
<http://www.learnthenet.com/english/html/20how.htm>.

"How to Backup Outlook Express (OE) Email." iopus.com.
<http://www.iopus.com/guides/oe-backup.htm>.

"Information and Resources for Unix and Linux Systems." A.P. Lawrence.
<http://aplawrence.com/SCOFAQ/scotec1.html>.

Jones, Bruce. "Ideology and Literacy." Critical Computer Literacy.
<http://communication.ucsd.edu/bjones/comp_lit_paper.html>.

McKay, Dawn Rosenberg. "Career Planning: Computer Literacy." about.com.
<http://careerplanning.about.com/od/importantskills/a/comp_literacy.htm>.

"Networkng Definitions." WhatIs.Com.
<http://searchnetworking.techtarget.com/sDefinition/0,,sid7_gci881593,00.html>.

Sisco, Michael. "How to calculate and convey the true cost of downtime." TechRepublic.com.
<http://techrepublic.com.com/5100-10878_11-1038783.html>.

"Statistics about Business Size." U.S. Census Bureau.
<http://www.census.gov/epcd/www/smallbus.html>.

Thurott, Paul. "OS Market Share: Microsoft Stomps the Competition." WindowsITPro.com.
<http://www.windowsitpro.com/Articles/Index.cfm?ArticleID=40481&DisplayTab=Article>.

Toigo, Jon William. di*saster RECOVERY planning – preparing for the unthinkable*. Upper Saddle River, NJ: Prentice Hall, 2003

"Top 10 Reasons to Use Windows Small Business Server 2003." Microsoft Corporation.
<http://www.microsoft.com/windowsserver2003/sbs/evaluation/top.mspx>.

"Total Cost of Ownership." Wikipedia.
<http://en.wikipedia.org/wiki/Total_cost_of_ownership>.

"Using Email Effectively." Passion Computing.
<http://www.passioncomputing.com.au/Web_Copywriting/Using_email.aspx>.

Wallace, Michael and Lawrence Webber. *The Disaster Recovery Handbook: A Step-by-Step Plan to Ensure Business Continuity and Protection*. New York: AMACOM, 2004.

INDEX

A+
  Defined 28
ABC 62, 70, 89, 108
Accounting Firm 23
Acrobat 94
address book 88
Administrative Handbook 74
Application Software
  Defined 48
Archival Backup Copy .. See ABC
asset list
  Defined 67
Asset Tracking 67
attachment 42, 43
backup 33, 47, 53, 55, 62, 65, 88, 100, 116, 118, 143
backup log 101, 119
bandwidth 24
bare metal
  Defined 105
battery 119, 120, 121, 124
BHO 138
  Defined 94
Bookkeeper 29
browser .. 6, 93, 95, 97, 118, 132, 138
Browser Helper Object. See BHO
byte
  Defined 4
capital purchase 31
case sensitive 63, 64, 81
  Defined 63
CCNA
  Defined 28
CCNP
  Defined 28
CDP .... See Continuous Data Protection
CD-ROM

  Defined 5
Changing File Associations
  How-To 66
charitable donation 114
Cisco 28
CLE
  Defined 28
Clean-Mail 92
CNA
  Defined 28
CNE
  Defined 28
Comptia 28
Computer
  Case 2
  Hard Drive 4
  Memory 3
  Motherboard 3
  Network Interface 4
  Parallel Interface 4
  Power Supply 3
  Processor 3
  Serial Interface 4
  USB Interface 4
  Video Display Interface 4
computer literacy
  Defined 44
Continuous Data Protection .. 104
cookie 93, 97
Cost per User Annually .... See CPUA
CPU
  Defined 3
CPUA
  Defined 32
Credit Card 98
decibel 75
Device Drivers .... See Drivers
DHCP 59

154

Defined 11
Disaster Prevention
   Defined 110
Disaster Recovery 25, 108
DNS 139
domain name 81, 86
   Defined 80
Domain Name Services 139
down time 115
Down Time 117, 129
Down Time Calculator 18
driver
   Defined 7
DSL 9, 136, 148
DVD 5, 69, 70, 102, 104, 108, 113, 119, 124, 143, 144, 146
DVD-ROM
   Defined 5
E-Commerce 84
e-mail ... 8, 15, 16, 37, 42, 43, 44, 45, 53, 73, 80, 85, 86, 87, 88, 89, 90, 91, 97, 98, 102, 112, 128, 139, 143
E-mail
   Defined 85
emergency response 23
employee handbook 43
Event Log 118
File Extensions
   Table List 65
file server4, 9, 16, 37, 55, 58, 62, 69, 88, 89, 90, 100, 103, 104, 105, 106, 112, 115, 116, 117, 118, 120, 127, 130, 143, 144, 145
   Defined 8
fire extinguisher 110
Firefox 95, 97
firewall 11, 60
Firewall
   Defined 9
five 9s rule

Defined 83
folder .. 13, 43, 58, 61, 62, 68, 70, 88, 89, 90, 91, 140
   Defined 61
FTP 64
gateway 11, 59
   Defined 9
generator 121, 122
GLBA 55
GoDaddy 81
Google 80, 142
grammar 87
Hard Drive
   Defined 4
hardware 2
helpdesk 26, 34, 50, 56, 68
HIPAA 55, 75, 76
   Defined 147
hot fix
   Defined 6
Hub
   Defined 9
human cost 40
Human Resources 43
Identity theft 112
IHateSpam .... *See* SPAM
Inbox 89
incremental backup
   Defined 104
industry certification 26
Internet 8, 80
Internet Explorer 6, 46, 93, 94, 95, 97
Internet Merchant Account 84
IP address 11, 59, 81, 136
ISP ... 9, 24, 54, 59, 81, 137, 139, 147
IT policy
   Defined 42
IT training 45, 47
keyboard 114
   Defined 5

155

label printer 75
   Defined 55
Large Network
   Defined 16
Lavasoft 93
Linux 28, 64, 117, 152
Local IT firm
   Defined 23
mail order 21, 52, 102, 103
maintenance
   budget 31
MCP
   Defined 28
MCSA
   Defined 28
MCSE
   Defined 28
Medium Network
   Defined 16
Microsoft Certified Professional
   .... *See* MCP
Microsoft Certified Systems
   Administrator .... *See* MCSA
Microsoft Certified Systems
   Engineer .... *See* MCSE
Microsoft Exchange 88
mirror failure 37
Modem
   Defined 9
Monitor 114
   Defined 5
Mouse
   Defined 5
Mozilla 93, 95, 97
Mozilla Firefox 93
MP3 .... 5, 113
MSCONFIG 133
My Documents 62
NAS .... *See* Network Attached
   Storage
Network
   Defined 2

Network Attached Storage 105
Network+
   Defined 28
notebook .. 22, 73, 109, 120, 124,
125
Notebook 123
Novell 28
Office Manager 29
off-site 26, 36, 44, 56, 59, 62, 67,
68, 69, 70, 71, 72, 101, 102,
105, 108, 109, 119
Online Catalog 84
online sales 84
Online Shopping Cart 84
on-site 21, 23, 36, 40, 55, 59, 69,
78, 79, 102, 108, 123, 130
Opera 93
Operating System
   Defined 6
Operations Supervisor 29
Outlook 143
Outlook Express 88, 90, 143
outside vendor 23
   Defined 23
P2P .... *See* Peer
password .. 36, 55, 56, 57, 59, 73,
74, 95, 97, 98, 99, 102, 112,
129, 139, 148
passwords 43
Passwords 98
patch 41
PC
   Defined 2
PDA
   Defined 4
peer
   Defined 115
peripheral
   Defined 10
Personal Folders 143, 144
Plant Manager 29
Pop-up 95

PortOne 92
Power
  Defined 120
PPPoE 59
printer driver .... 42, *See* Driver
Printer Driver 141
PTF
  Defined 6
Rack mount 76
RAID-5 116
RAM 124
  Defined 3
recipient 85, 86, 87, 145
reciprocal agreement
  Defined 109
Registry 135
remote access 74
repository 115
restore points 134
retail store 23
Return on Investment ..... 34, *See* ROI
RJ-45 9
ROI 34, 148
  Defined 35
router 11, 60, 67, 114
Router 54, 59, 148
  Defined 9
Safari 93
Sarbanes-Oxley 55
SEC Rule 17a-4 55
Security+
  Defined 28
Service Pack 70
  Defined 6
Service Release
  Defined 6
Shareware
  Defined 51
Shopping Cart 84
Skill Set Profile
  Defined 46

small business
  Defined 12
small business owner ..... viii, 1, 2, 12, 19, 21, 22, 25, 29, 30, 31, 34, 73, 80, 83, 108
  Defined 12
Small Network
  Defined 16
SMTP 59, 139
software 6
  Defined 2
software upgrade 41
spam 85, 88, 92, 96
Spam
  Defined 92
spyware 37, 93, 96, 128, 132
switch 114
Switch
  Defined 9
Tape Backup
  Defined 8
tape drive 100, 103, 108, 110
TCO .... *See* Total Cost of Ownership
TCP-IP
  Defined 11
Technician Certification 26, 28
TELNET 64
terminated employee 111
thermometer 110
TLD
  Defined 81
Top Level Domain .... *See* TLD
Top Ten E-Mail Rules 87
Total Cost of Ownership
  Defined 34
training center 24
United States trademark 81
Universal Serial Bus 4
Unix 64, 117, 152
UPS 10, 76, 77, 78, 118, 119, 120, 121, 130, 149

157

UPS Device
  Defined 10
uptime 24, 82, 83
URL
  Defined 81
USB Device
  Defined 10
User Profile
  Defined 56
Vertical Market
  Defined 24
vertical market application 49
  Defined 48
virus 36, 43, 73, 96, 105, 117, 119, 130, 131

virus software 43, 131
VPN 28, 112
war parking
  Defined 73
Web Designer 83
web site 70, 81, 82
WEP 73
Windows 2000 .... 6, 37, 128
Windows XP 3, 6, 20, 46, 116, 123, 142
Workstation Imaging
  Defined 105
Yahoo 80